# Colors of the Web

*Friends Forever*

**Jeanie Breedwell**

Colors of the Web
Copyright © 2021 by Jeanie Breedwell

All rights reserved. No part of this publication may be reproduced, distributed, or transmitted in any form or by any means, including photocopying, recording, or other electronic or mechanical methods, without the prior written permission of the author, except in the case of brief quotations embodied in critical reviews and certain other non-commercial uses permitted by copyright law.

ISBN
978-1-956161-12-0 (Paperback)
978-1-956161-11-3 (eBook)

DID YOU LIKE SCHOOL? YES, I DID. I HAD LOTS OF FRIENDS WHAT ABOUT BOYFRIENDS?
YES, THEM TO DID YOUR DADDY KNOWS ABOUT THEM NO, I WOULD NOT TELL HIM.
WHAT ABOUT YOUR MAMA? NO, I DID NOT TELL HER EATHER.
SO, YOU KEEP IT A SECRET, YES, I DID; IT WAS NOTHING, JUST A CRUST.
THAT IS ALL. WILL DID YOU GO OUT WITH ANYONE? NOT UNTIL I GOT SEVENTEEN.
THEY WOULD NOT LET ME DATE,
SAID I WAS TOO YOUNG DID YOU FEEL THAT WAY? NO, I DID NOT! WANTED TO SEE BOYS.
WHEN I WAS FIFTEEN, BUT YOUR GRANDMA WOULD NOT LET ME.


SO HOW OLD WERE YOU WHEN YOU MET MY DADDY?
I WAS TWENTY, AND YOU CAME ALONG AFTER WE GOT MARRIED, WE WENT TOGETHER.
ONE YEAR MAMA DID NOT WANT ME TO GET MARRIED AT TWENTY, SO YOU HAD TO DO WHAT GRANDMA SAID?
YES, THEN HOW LONG DID I COME ALONG WE WERE MARRIED FOR ABOUT FOUR MONTHS. YOU CAME ALONG.

WHY DID YOU NOT HAVE MORE KIDS LIKE A SON? TO BE NAME AFTER DADDY.
WELL, I COULD NOT HAVE ANY MORE, THE DOCTOR SAID.

WE TRIED, BUT THAT IS IT NOW, LITTLE GIRL, YOU NEED TO CLEAN YOUR ROOM.
OK, I WILL.
DID YOU EVER FIND OUT ABOUT DADDY? AND HIS GROWING UP.
IT WAS OK. I GUESS HE NEVER SAID GRANDPA STILL LIVING NO HONEY. HE IS GONE; HE WAS SICK LOTS.
I KNOW MAMA MISSING HIM SO MUCH. YES, MAMA, I AM SURE SHE DOES. NOT YOU NEED TO DO WHAT I ASKED YOU TO DO.
AND QUIT ASKING SO MANY QUESTING OK MAMA, I WILL STOP YOU BETTER. I GOT ALL MY ANSWERS, BUT I NEED TO CLEAN MY ROOM...
AND I NEED TO ASK YOU SOMETHING?
OK, WHAT IS IT LATER, MAMA? I WILL LET YOU KNOW AFTER I CLEAN MY ROOM. OK, DEAR.

NOW I THINK I WILL CLEAN MY ROOM. I HAVE SOMETHING TO ASKED MAMA. ABOUT SUE AND ME.
SO, CINDY BEGINS TO CLEAN HER ROOM. I WILL PUT THIS HERE MY DOLL GOES HERE

MY SHOES GOES HERE, AND MY BOOKS GOES HERE. MY SHEETS GO HERE. AND MY BAG GOES HERE.

MY DRESS HUNG UP. I WILL NEED TO GET ME A CHAIR TO STAND UP IN TO PUT MY DRESS IN THE CLOSET.

HERE IS MY TOYS. I WILL PUT THEM IN MY TOY BOX, AND THIS GOES HERE I WILL. PUT THIS HERE.
I AM ALMOST THOUGH I CAN GO TALK TO MAMA IT IS ALL CLEAN UP NOW. MAMA, I HAVE CLEAN MY ROOM.

OK DEAR, NOW WE CAN TALK, MAMA CAN WE I HAVE WANTED TO FIND. OUT ABOUT THIS FOR SO LONG, OK LITTLE GIRL.
WHAT IS IT.

MAMA, WHEN ME AND SUE ARE PLAYING AROUND, THE OTHER KIDS MAKE FUN AT US.

IT IS OK, HONEY, YOU DO NOT PAY ANY MIND TO THE KIDS, BUT MAMA, IT ISSUE BLACK AND ME WHITE.
WHY DO THEY MAKE FUN OF US? I DO NOT UNDERSTAND IT IS OK; MAMA GOD DID NOT MAKE A MISTAKE?

NO, DEAR GOD DOES NOT MAKE MISTAKES WILL WHY THEY HAVE GOT TO BE SO MEAN. HONEY, I

DO NOT KNOW. I WILL ASKED MRS ODELL MAYBE SHE CAN HELP ME.

HONEY, SHE WILL TELL YOU THE SAME AS ME SHE WILL? YES, DEAR, SHE WILL. SUE IS MY FRIEND, AND SHE WILL ALWAYS BE.
THAT IS RIGHT, HONEY,

IT HURTS US WHEN THEY MAKE FUN. I KNOW, HONEY, BUT I DO NOT HAVE THE ANSWER FOR YOU,
OK, MAMA, I WILL FIND OUT WHEN I GET OLDER YES, I GUESS YOU CAN.
IT IS SOMETHING I DO NOT HAVE AN ANSWER FOR.

I WILL; GO PLAY WITH MY DOLL NOW, MAMA OK DEAR, I HAVE LOTS OF TOYS. TO PLAY WITH OK DEAR, YOU DO THAT.

IT IS SO PRETTY, MY DOLL, YES DEAR, IT IS. WE WILL HAVE LUNCH SOON. OK.

MAMA, I WILL BE IN MY ROOM. I WILL CALL YOU WHEN IT IS READY.

OK, MAMA, I WILL BE PLAYING WITH MY TOYS. SANTA BROUGHT ME FOR CHRISTMAS. OK, DEAR.

WILL I DID NOT GET ANY ANSWER FROM MAMA.
I WILL TRY ANOUGHT TIME.

I REMBER SUE AND ME PLAYING TOGETHER, AND
SHE WOULD CRY. I WOULD ASK HER WHY,

SHE NEVER TOLD ME WHY I ASKED BUT NEVER
GOT AN ANSWER.

ONE DAY MAMA AND SUE MAMA CARRIED US
SHOPPING WE WERE PLAYING. THE WHITE KIDS
LOOK.

AT ME AND SUE REAL HARD, I JUST LOOK BACK,
BUT SUE CRIED. SHE WAS UPSET

I PUT MY ARMS AROUND HER, AND SHE WAS OK,
BUT I COULD SEE IT HURT. HER SO BAD.

MANY TIMES, WHEN WE WENT PLACES, SUE
WOULD CRY.

SHE KNEW THEY WERE MAKING FUN OF HER.

WE WENT OUT IN THE WOODS, AND WE PLAY, SO
NO ONE WAS THER ACCEPT US.

AND SHE WAS OK WITH THAT SO WHEN WE WANTED TO PLAY THAT. IS WHAT WE DID.

FIND US A PLACE IN THE WOODS WHERE THERE WOULD BE JUST.

ONE DAY CINDY AND SUE WENT TO THE STORE TO GET SOME GROCERS. MAMA, LET'S GET SOME CANDY FOR SUE AND ME.
OK, I WILL, AND I WILL GET SOME APPLES FOR YOU ALL TO. YES, MAMA, THAT IS GOOD

NOW YOU GO LOOK AT SOMETHING ELSE WHILE I GET MY GROCERS.

OK, MAMA, I WILL. I SEE SOME CAKE AND COOKIES TO. NO CAKE. AND COOKIES FOR YOU.

OK, MAMA, I WANT TO ASK YOU FOR THAT JUST CANDY.

OK, DEAR, I WILL GET IT FOR YOU;

I WANT TO BUY SOMETHING SAID SUE OK I WILL GET YOU AND CINDY SOME CANDY

MAMA IS GETTING US SOME CANDY. OK, WHAT ABOUT NUTS, YES. MAMA.

THAT WILL BE GOOD.

WILL I AM READY TO GO HOME, ARE YOU MRS ODELL?

YES, I AM.

MAMA LETS GO BY THE GRAVEYARD. I WANT TO SEE MY GRANDFATHER GRAVE.
OK, DEAR, TOMORROW.

WE NEED TO GET OUR GROCERS HOME. I HAVE ICE CREAM IN MY BAG.
WE NEED TO GET HOME NOW.

OK, MAMA, LET'S GO. I WILL GET SOME CANDY.
YOU DID GET IT, MAMA. YES, I DID.
AND SUE MAMA GOT SOME FOR YOU GIRLS.

WILL WE ARE HOME LETS HELP MRS ODELL WITH HER GROCERS.

IT IS OK; I WILL GET THEM.
LET ME GIVE CINDY SOME CANDY THAT IS OK

WE WILL GIVE IT TO THEM LATER.
OK, MAMA, WE CAN WAIT.

WILL I NEED TO GET THESE GROCERS UP IN THE CABIN AND THE FROZEN?
ONE IN THE FREEZER. OK, MAMA, I CAN HELP SEE YOU LATER SUE YES THANKS MRS WHITE FOR TAKEN US TO THE STORE.
WELCOME.

WILL I HAVE GOT TO GO GET MY GROCERS HOME NOW?
YES, MAMA, WE DO.

WILL WE ARE HOME YOUR DADDY WILL BE HERE SOON.
YES, MAMA, HE WILL.

YOU HELP MAMA TO PUT THE GROCERS UP.
OK, MAMA, I WILL.

I HAVE GOT TO GET MY SUPPER DONE.
YES; I KNOW MAMA. I CAN HELP MAMA.

NO, I TOLD YOU THAT YOU WERE TO LITTLE, REMEMBER.

YES, MAMA, I KNOW I AM SO TIRED. I THINK I WILL SIT DOWN. NOW.

OK, MAMA, YOU CAN TALK TO ME NOW; DO NOT GET ON THAT SAME.
THING YOU WERE TALKING ABOUT EARLY.

I WON'T, MAMA, BUT COULD YOU TELL ME HOW YOU WERE. IN SCHOOL.

OK, WHAT DO YOU WANT TO KNOW? DID YOU MAKE GOOD?

IN SCHOOL ON YOUR SPELLING AND HISTORY BOOKS?
YES, I THINK SO

HOW DO YOU KNOW ABOUT THAT? I SAW IT ON TV, OH.
WHAT ABOUT YOUR REPORT CARD?

YES, I DID, OK, BUT YOU ARE TOO YOUNG TO ASKED THEM, KIND OF QUESTIONS

I KNOW, MAMA, SOME THINGS I GUESS YOU DO. TO SMART.
HERE COMES YOUR DADDY.

UP IN THE YARD, GO LET HIM IN. SMART THING OK MAMA DADDY.

MY LITTLE GIRL.

YES, DID YOU BRING ME SOMETHING? LET'S SEE, IS IT IN THAT POCKET?
ARE THIS POCKET.

HERE IT IS, CANDY HONEY, SHE HAS CANDY I GOT TODAY, OK CINDY.

YOU WILL PUT IT AWAY UNTIL MOM SAYS YOU CAN HAVE IT.

OK, DADDY, SO YOU ALL WENT TO THE STORE?
YES, AND MRS. ODELL AND SUE WENT WITH US.

WE HAD A GOOD TIME DADDY, MAMA, AND ME ARE GOING TO THE GRAVEYARD TOMORROW.

WHY BECAUSE I WANT TO GO SEE GRANDPA GRAVE.
OK, IF YOU AND MOM WANTS TO GO.

SUPPER WILL BE A LITTLE LATE, JOE. I WAS SO TIRED WHEN WE GOT HOME I SAT DOWN FOR A WHILE.

OK, YOU REST AM NOT IN A HURRY TO EAT. I AM OK NOW. I WILL GO GET SUPPER READY.

OK, DEAR, HE KISS HER ON THE SIDE OF THE FACE. I WILL GO WATCH. THE NEWS

OK, IT WILL BE READY SOON MAMA I WILL GO PLAY WITH MY TOYS.
NOW.

MAMA WILL CALL ME WHEN IT IS READY DADDY YES DEAR CAN I HAVE A FEW MINUTES OF YOUR TIME?

YES, WHAT DO YOU WANT? I WANT TO KNOW WHY KIDS LAUGHT. AT SUE AND ME /

WHAT DO YOU MEAN CINDY WILL WHEN WE PLAY TOGETHER? THEY MAKE FUN AT US.

WE ARE LITTLE GIRLS JUST LIKE THEM, BUT I KNOW GOD DID NOT MAKE.

A MISTAKE DID HE DADDY NO CINDY GOD KNEW WHAT HE WAS DOING BUT DADDY.

WHY WOULD THEY MAKE FUN AT US BECAUSE WE ARE WHITE AND BLACK.

IT IS THE WAY KIDS DO NOW DAYS DO NOT WORRY WHAT. KIDS SAY.

THEY ARE JUST MEAN THAT IS ALL I KNOW IT DADDY, BUT I FEEL. SORRY FOR SUE.

SHE CRYS WHEN THEY DO HER THAT WAY. AND I JUST LOOK AT THEM. I DO NOT CARE.

THEY MAKE ME MAD AND SUE CRYS DADDY, WHY CAN'T PEOPLE GET ALONG?

I DO NOT KNOW, CINDY, IT IS BAD IN OUR WORLD; YOU PRAY FOR THEM; THAT IS WHAT

JESUS SAID TO DO.

DADDY, THAT IS A GOOD ANSWER. I WILL DO THAT THE NEXT TIME THEY TREAT US BAD.

OK, CINDY, THAT WILL DO. GOD WILL ANSWER YOUR PRAYS YOU WILL SEE.
NOW LET ME LOOK AT THE WEATHER IT LOOKS LIKE WE MAY GET SOME BAD WEATHER.

RUTH COME HERE OK; I AM COMING WHAT IS IT? IT MAY BE BAD WEATHER COMING OUR WAY.

YES, I THINK YOU ARE RIGHT; IT DOES LOOK BAD IT MAY BE HERE. TOMORROW.
YOU MAY NEED TO STAY HOME WE WILL SEE DID YOUR MOTHER CALL YOU.

YES, SHE DID IS SHE COMING YES, THE DOCTOR SAID SHE COULD DRIVE

SO, SHE WILL LEAVE NEXT WEEK ABOUT TIME TO GET. YOUR VACATION, YES, THAT IS RIGHT

RUTH, I THINK I WILL CALL MAMA AND SEE IF SHE WANTS ME TO FLY UP THERE.
AND RIDE WITH HER, SO SHE DOES NOT HAVE TO BE BY HERSELF. ARE YOU SURE?

YES, I AM. I WILL BE WORRIED ABOUT HER BY HER SELF ON THAT LONG TRIP.
ON A FLIGHT IT WILL ONLY BE FIVE HOURS, OK, YOU KNOW BEST. CINDY GET DADDY THE PHONE.
OK DAD, HERE IT IS LET ME RING HER NUMBER HELLO MAMA YES. SON, ARE YOU OK?
YES, WHY DO YOU ASKED WILL IT IS ONLY FOUR O'CLOCK HERE. OH, I FORGOT.
WILL SINCE I GOT YOU UP, I WANTED TO KNOW IF I FLEW UP THERE? WOULD IT BE OK?
THEN I COULD HELP YOU DRIVE DOWN HERE. ARE YOU SURE THAT IS WHAT YOU WANT?

SON, I WILL BE OK I AM LEAVING HERE WEDNESDAY, BUT MAMA, IF YOU WAIT, THAT IS WHEN I TAKE MY VACATION.

OK, SO, IF THAT IS WHAT YOU WANT, MAMA, I WILL LEAVE HERE WEDNESDAY.

THAT WILL START MY VACATION. SORRY, I WOKE YOU UP. BUT I WANTED TO GET YOU BEFORE YOU LEFT.

OK, SON, YOU COME ON. I WILL GET EVERYTHING READY, ARE YOU TELLING TONY?

I GUESS I WILL CALL HIM. SEE YOU WEDNESDAY; OK MAMA, LOVE YOU BYE.

ARE YOU GOING? YES, I WILL LEAVE HERE WEDNESDAY MORNING. TODAY IS SATURDAY.

OVER THE WEEKEND, YOU WILL NEED TO PACK ME A BAG, JUST A FEW. THINGS.

DADDY, YOU ARE GOING TO FLORIDA. YES, DEAR GRANDMA IS COMING HERE.

OH BOY, I WILL GET TO SEE GRANDMA IT HAS BEEN SO LONG. I WONT TO CALL SUE.

TELL HER SHE CAN SEE GRANDMA; SHE SAW HER ONE TIME NOW THIS IS GREAT.

MAMA TAKE ME DOWN TO SEE SUE WE CAN WALK IT ISN'T THAT FAR

OK, MAMA.

ARE YOU READY? YES, CINDY JOE, WE WILL BE BACK IN A LITTLE WHILE.

OK, RUTH MAMA, THE LORD GAVE US SOME PRETTY WEATHER, YES, BUT THERE IS STORMY WEATHER.

COMING, I SAW IT ON THE NEWS, BUT RIGHT NOW, IT IS OK, YES, MAMA. WE ARE HERE.
LET ME KNOCK ON THE DOOR I AM COMING WILL COME ON IN SUE CINDY IS HERE.

COMING MAMA CINDY WANTED TO TELL SUE SOMETHING OK SUE DADDY IS GOING TO GET GRANDMA.

IN FLORIDA WHEN NEXT WEDNESDAY, HE IS FLYING DOWN THERE, SO SHE WON'T TO BE BY HERSELF.

COMING TO STAY WITH US FOR A WHILE. I REMEMBER HER GOOD. YES, I THOUGHT YOU DID.

IT HAS BEEN A LONG TIME MRS WHITE WILL HE BE GONE VERY LONG? I HOPE NOT. WILL I KNOW

YOU BOTH WILL MISS HIM YES, WE WILL, MRS ODELL? WILL WE WILL BE HERE IF YOU NEED US.

THANK YOU, BUT WE WILL BE OK I WILL TAKE MY HUSBAND TO THE AIRPORT SO HE CAN LEAVE HERE.

WILL I GUESS WE WILL GO HOME? I HAVE SOME THINGS I NEED TO DO BEFORE WEDNESDAY.

BYE SUE SEE YOU SOON SEE YOU MISS ODELL, YES YOU TO.

TELL YOUR HUSBAND I WILL PRAY FOR HIM TO HAVE A SAFE TRIP, OK


 THANK.YOU.

GOD WILL BE WITH THEM I AM SURE .SO CINDY AND HER MOTHER LEFT GOING HOME.
WE ARE BACK JOE MRS ODELL SAID SHE WOULD PRAY FOR YOU WHILE YOU ARE GONE.

HOW IS EVERYONE DOING OK I GUESS WE WERE TELLING THEM ABOUT THE TRIP.
I DID NOT SEE HER HUSBAND HE MAY HAVE BEEN GONE MAMA MAY I HAVE A LITTLE OF YOURS AND DADDY TIME?
SURE, WHAT IS ON YOUR MIND LITTLE GIRL? WHEN I WAS BORN, HOW WAS IT.
HOW WAS WHAT? THE WEATHER MAMA WELL IT WAS RAINING AND

YOUR DADDY.

HAD TO FIGHT THE TRAFFIC GOING TO THE HOSPITAL AND THE RED LIGHTS STAY RED.
SO, THE CAR STOP AND YOUR DADDY HAD TO GO TO THE HOUSE AND CALL SOMEONE.

TO COME TAKE ME TO THE HOSPITAL BUT I DID NOT MAKE IT BECAUSE YOU WERE BORN IN THE CAR YOUR.DADDY WAS THE ONE THAT BROUGHT YOU INTO THIS WORLD. WITH A FEW ANGELS HELPING. HIM.
HE DID A GOOD JOB WHY DID YOU ASKED THAT BECAUSE I SAW THE BIRTH CERTIFICATE AND IT SAID.

I WAS BORN IN A CAR. WHERE DID YOU GET IT? YOU NEED TO STOP LOOKING FOR THINGS.
SO THAT WAS OUR CAR YES, I DID NOT MAKE IT TO THE HOSPITAL YOUR DADDY WAS IN THE ARMY.
HE DID THINGS SO HE KNEW HOW TO BRING YOU INTO THE WORLD. THAT IS WHAT HE DID,

THANKS DADDY YOU WERE MY DOCTOR YES, I WAS I HAD TO NO ONE. WAS THERE THAT KNEW ANYTHING.

WILL ARE YOU HAPPY NOW TO KNOW YOUR MAMA HAD YOU IN A CAR?
BUT YOU COULD NOT HELP IT.

YES, THAT IS RIGHT, BUT YOU ARE HERE YOU WERE SO PRETTY SAID HER DADDY.

I WAS YES YOU WERE RUTH GO GET THE PICTURES AND SHOW THEM TO HER.
OK I WILL HERE THEY ARE LOOK AT YOU THIS WAS AT THE HOSPITAL. PRETTY MAMA.
YES, YOU WERE AND STILL ARE. THANKS MAMA HER MAMA PUT HER ARMS AROUND HER LITTLE GIRL.

NOW I HAVE THINGS TO DO SO YOU CAN PLAY WITH YOUR TOYS. ARE TALK TO YOUR DADDY.
NOW CINDY DADDY HAS GOT TO CLEAN THE YARD I WANT EVERYTHING NICE.
FOR YOUR GRANDMA SHE LIKES CLEAN THINGS OK DOCTOR DADDY FUNNY HE GRABS HER AND HUGS HER NOW.
YOU GO PLAY FOR DADDY I WILL I NEED TO CLEAN MY ROOM BEFORE. GRANDMA COMES.
CINDY COME HERE OK MAMA WHAT DO YOU WANT? YOUR BIRTHDAY IS SOON WHAT DO YOU WANT?

MAMA I WOULD LIKE A BIKE FOR SUE AND ME TO RIDE. WE ARE TO YOUNG. FOR SCHOOL.

SO, COULD YOU GET US A BIKE? OK I WILL GO LOOK FOR ONE. WHAT COLOR BLUE AND FOR SUE GREEN OK NOW YOU BE NICE. AND WE WILL SEE.


IS THAT ALL YES SO GO PLAY NOW OK MAMA I WILL THE WEEKEND WENT BY FAST
IT WAS MONDAY MORNING HER DADDY WAS LEAVING FOR WORK BYE CINDY BYE DADDY.

WHAT ARE WE GOING TO DO TODAY MAMA?
LET'S GET THE THINGS FOR YOUR DADDY PACK.
HE IS LEAYING IN TWO DAYS MAMA I WILL MISS I WILL TO HE HAS BEEN WITH US
IT HAS BEEN A LONG TIME SINCE HE HAS BE AWAY FROM US. YES MAMA.
MAMA LOOK, SOMEONE IS MOVING IN NEXT DOOR I SEE TO LITTLE GIRLS.

YES, AND TO LITTLE BOYS THEY ARE OLDER THAN ME. HOW DO YOU KNOW THAT?
BECAUSE THEY ARE BIGGER THAN ME ARE SUE. I WANT TO WELCOME THEM IN OUR NEIGHBORHOOD.
CAN I MAMA YES IF YOU WANT TO OK I WILL SO CINDY GOES NEXT DOOR.

HI I AM CINDY, I COME TO WELCOME YOU HERE WHAT YOUR NAME? I AM PEGGY AND MY BABY SISTER IS TAMMY AND MY BROTHERS ARE TONY AND GARY NICE TO MEET YOU ALL.
MY MAMA IS SANDY AND MY DAD IS BUCH WE ARE THE JONES.

YOU ARE NEW HERE YES; WE CAME FROM FLORIDA REALY THAT IS WHERE MY GRANDMA LIVES.


MY MOTHER IS RUTH AND MY DADDY IS JOE WE ARE THE WHITE NICE. TO MEET YOU WE LIVE NEXT DOOR IF YOU AND YOUR SISTER.
I WANT TO COME OVER AND PLAY SOMETIMES.

OK WHEN WE GET SETTLE IN, MAYBE WE CAN COME OVER. THAT WOULD BE NICE.
YOU DO NOT GO TO SCHOOL DO YOU KNOW I AM ONLY FIVE YEARS OLD. BUT YOU ARE SO SMART.
THANK YOU WE ARE OLDER I AM SEVEN AND MY SISTER IS FIVE AND MY BROTHERS ARE EIGHT HE IS AND THE OTHER ONE IS FOUR HE IS YOUNGER.
WILL I HAVE GOT TO GO SEE YOU LATER OK SO CINDY LEFT MAMA SHE CALL.
BEFORE SHE OPEN THE DOOR, THE PEOPLE ARE SO NICE. GOOD THE ONE

HER NAME IS PEGGY AND HER BABY SISTER IS TAMMY TWO BOYS ARE TONY AND GARY THE JONES. THEY COME FROM FLORIDA WHERE GRANDMA LIVES IS THAT ALL THE

THE WEEK GOES BY FAST IT IS TIME FOR CINDY DADDY TO GO TO THE AIRPORT.

ARE YOU READY, RUTH I NEED TO BE THERE BY SEVEN MY FLIGHT WILL BE LEAVING?

I AM COMING IN THE CAR, DADDY I WILL MISS YOU SO MUCH ME TO LITTLE GIRL.

RUTH, YOU MAKE SURE YOU PUT SOME OIL IN YOUR CAR OK AND I WILL CALL.
YOU WHEN I GET THERE LISTEN FOR THE PHONE I WILL IT WILL TAKE US.
SOMETIME TO GET BACK, I WILL FEEL YOU IN AFTER I TALK TO MAMA. OK.
I WILL PRAY FOR YOU DADDY SAID CINDY AS SHE HELT ON TO HER DADDY.

OK NOW LET GO I NEED TO TELL YOUR MAMA BYE OK DADDY AS THE TEARS FALL.
FROM HER EYES, NO WATER WORKDS OK DADDY WILL CALL YOU WHEN I GET TO FLORIDA. YOU TAKE CARE OF MAMA WHILE DADDY IS. GONE.

AND RUTH, YOU TAKE CARE OF YOUR SELF I LOVE YOU BOOTH YES SAID HIS WIFE.
WE LOVE YOU TO GOT TO GO NO DADDY YES GOT TO GET HER RUTH COME ON CINDY.

DADDY WILL RETURN.
WITH GRANDMOTHER YOU WILL SEE OK YES MAMA I DO BUT I MISS DADDY.
HE IS GOING SOUTH NOW, MAMA LETS GO GET SOMETHING TO EAT. OK WE WILL.
LATER IT IS TO EARLY NOW DON'T YOU WANT TO REST FIRST? I DID NOT SLEEP TO MUCH.
LAST NIGHT IT IS SO LONESOME HERE BEFORE I GO INTO THE HOUSE.

LOOK MAMA THE KIDS NEXT DOOR ARE UP I WILL WAVE AT THEM. THEY WEVE BACK.
MAMA WHAT ARE WE GOING TO DO WHILE DADDY GONE? HE WILL BE BACK.
SOON HE WILL BE BACK VERY SOON. YOU CAN CALL SUE SHE CAN SPEND THE NIGHT,
NO MAMA I WILL JUST PLAY NOW I DO NOT FEEL LIKE COMPANY. OK DEAR.


I AM GOING TO LAY DOWN NOW WAIT ON DADDY CALL YES MAMA ME TO.

MAMA THERE IS A KNOCK AT THE DOOR OK DEAR YOU CAN ANSWER IT

MAMA IT IS THE GIRLS NEXT DOOR WHO WANTS ME TO PLAY WITH THEM?
OK BUT STAY IN YOUR YARD.
THEY CAN PLAY HERE TO CINDY DO NOT GO OUT OF YOUR YARD. OK MAMA.
PEGGY, I HAVE GOT TO PLAY IN MY YARD MAMA SAID. OK I WILL GO
GET SOME OF MY TOYS.

I WILL BE RIGHT BACK OK CINDY. SO, CINDY GOT SOME OF HER TOYS HERE YOU CAN PLAY WITH THIS.
AND TAMMY YOU PLAY WITH THIS THANK YOU MY DADDY LEFT THIS MORNING.
GOING TO FLORIDA BUT HE WILL BE BACK SOON HE IS BRINGING MY GRANDMA BACK.

YOUR GRANDMA LIVES IN FLORIDA? YES, SHE IS COMING FOR A VISIT. MY DADDY.
WENT TO HELP HER DRIVE BACK HERE. MY GRANDMA HAS NOT DROVE IN ALONG.
TIME, I MISS MY DADDY WE MAY NOT STAY HERE LONG WE MAY BE GOING BACK TO FLORIDA.

WHY WILL MY MOM AND DAD BROKE U PUT DADDY WANTS US BACK

BUT I THOUGHT THE MAN WE SAW WHEN YOU WERE MOVING IN WAS YOUR DADDY.

NO, THAT WAS MY UNCLE JACK HE LIVES HERE SO HE HELP US. FIND A HOUSE.

BUT MAMA WANTS TO GO BACK WHEN I THINK TOMORROW DADDY. IS COMING AFTER US.

SO, SAD I LIKE YOU PEOPLE WE LIKE YOU TO. BUT MAMA IS THE RULE HERE.

WE HAVE GOT TO FOLLOW HER WILL IT WAS NICE TO KNOW YOU ALL

WE CAN WRITE YOU AND CALL IF YOU WANT TO.

OK I WILL GIVE YOU MY NUMBER AND ADDRESS LET ME GO GET IT FROM MAMA.
I WILL BE RIGHT BACK .SO CINDY GOES INTO HER HOUSE MAMA YES CINDY.
THEM PEOPLE NEXT DOOR ARE MOVING WHY? IT IS A LONG STORY.
I WILL TELL YOU LATER THEY WANT MY NUMBER AND ADDRESS.
OK MAMA HERE IT IS.

THANKS MAMA CINDY RUSH OUT SIDE HERE IT IS PEGGY ABOUT THAT TIME.
THE CHILDREN MOTHER CALL THEM PEGGY YES MOTHER YOU ALL. COME HERE.
WE HAVE GOT TO PACK DADDY IS ON HIS WAY AFTER US BYE CINDY I WILL CALL YOU.
AND WRITE YOU OK BYE I NEED TO GO IN THE HOUSE SO THAT IS WHAT

CINDY DID.

MAMA HAS DADDY CALLED YET? NO NOT YET BUT SOON. OK MAMA. I HATE TO SEE THEM LEAVE MAMA THEY WERE VERY NICE.
IN A LITTLE CINDY HEAR THE PHONE HER MAMA ANSWER.
IT IS YOUR DADDY.
I SEE YOU MADE IT TO FLORIDA YES, I DID HOW IS YOUR MAMA DOING?
SHE IS OK.
SO, WHEN ARE YOU GOING TO LEAVE OUT IN A LITTLE WE SHOULD BE. THERE NO LATER THAN SUNDAY OK DEAR CAN I TALK TO MY DADDY? YES YOU CAN.
HERE IS YOUR LITTLE GIRL HELLO DADDY YOU WITH GRANDMA?
YES, I AM.
TELL HER HELLO FOR ME OK I WILL DADDY I HAD SOME FRIENDS. MOVED.
NEXT DOOR BUT THEY ARE MOVING GUESS WHERE THEY CAME FROM?
DADDY THEY ARE FROM FLORIDA.
THEY ARE YES DADDY GOT TO GO LITTLE GIRL LOVE YOU DADDY LOVE YOU LITTLE GIRL.
NOW GIVE THE PHONE BACK TO YOUR MAMA OK DADDY MAMA DADDY WANTS YOU.
OK DEAR I WILL SEE YOU WHEN I GET THERE LOVE YOU YOU TO JOE.

LOOK MAMA IT IS RAINING LET ME SEE IT WAS SUPPOSE TO BE BAD WEATHER. HERE.


IT IS GETTING BAD LET'S GO INSIDE THE WIND PICK UP MAMA. LES CALL DADDY.

NO, WE WILL BE OK MAYBE IT WILL GO AROUND MAMA IT IS GETTING WORSE.
YES, IT IS LISTEN LET ME LISTEN ON THE TV THERE IS A BAD STORM EVERYONE GET TO SHELTER NOW. OK CINDY LETS GO TO THE BASEMENT.

MAMA, I AM SCARED THE LORD WILL TAKE CARE OF US MAMA PRAY. OK LITTLE GIRL DEAR LORD KEEP US SAFE.
WHILE THE STORM IS BAD LISTEN, I DO NOT HEAR ANYTHING NOW.

LET'S GO AND SEE OK, MAMA, I DO NOT HEAR ANYTHING IT HAS STOP. YES, IT HAS.

WILL I KNEW IT WAS COMING IT WAS ON THE NEWS IT IS COOL NOW. YES, IT IS MAMA.
I WILL GO GET SUPPER DONE OK MAMA I HOPE SUE IS OK MAMA CALL SUE.

OK I WILL THE PHONE RINGS HELLO MRS ODELL ARE YOU ALL OK?
YES, WE ARE FINE.
THE STORM WENT OVER YES IT DID WE WERE IN THE BASEMENT. FOR A WHILE.
ARE YOU AND CINDY OK YES THANK YOU FOR ASKING.
GOOD IT WAS BAD BUT IT DID NOT TOUCH US AT THAT TIME I MISS
JOE SO MUCH.
AND CINDY WANTED TO CALL HIM I JUST PRAYED ME TO SAID SUE MAMA.

WILL I GUESS IT IS OVER YES, WE WILL TALK LATER MRS ODELL BYE.

THE NEXT DAY WAS FRIDAY YOUR DADDY CALL ME SAID THEY WERE ALMOST HERE.
IT IS GOOD WEATHER THERE AND THEY WERE DOING GOOD TIME. SHOULD BE HERE SATURDAY INSTEAD SUNDAY GOOD MAMA.
I WANT TO SEE DADDY AND GRANDMA.

THE DAY WAS UPON THEM FOR MR WHITE TO COME HOME. DADDY SHOULD BE HERE SOON.

SAID HER MAMA YES, HE WILL LET'S CLEAN UP THE HOUSE BEFORE. GRANDMA GETS HERE.
SHE CAN SLEEP IN THE GUEST ROOM I WILL GO PUT CLEAN SHEETS ON HER BED.
YOU GO GET GRANDMA HOUSE SHOES SHE LEFT HERE WHEN SHE VISIT

THE LAST TIME.
MAMA THEY ARE IN MY ROOM. OK GO BRING THEM TO ME. I WILL,
MAMA HERE THEY ARE PUT THEM UNDER HER BED. SHE WILL BE LOOKING FOR THEM.

SHE LIKES THEM SO MUCH. MAMA THEY IS A STRANGE CAR IN OUR DRIVE WAY.
LET ME SEE IT IS YOUR DADDY AND GRANDMA SO CINDY RAN TO HER DADDY.

DADDY SO GLAD TO SEE YOU. YOU COME HERE AND GIVE YOUR GRANDMA A BIG KISS.
DID YOU FIND GRANDMA HOUSE SHOES? YES, I DID THEY ARE IN YOUR ROOM.

HA RUTH SO GLAD TO SEE YOU SHE HUG HER NECK. YOU TO MAMA. WE HAVE YOUR ROOM READY.

AND WE FOUND YOUR HOUSE SHOES. GOOD I LEFT THEM HERE. WHEN I VISIT BEFORE.
WILL LET GET MAMA THINGS AND GO IN THE HOUSE.

OK LET ME CARRIED IN MY GRANDMA BAG IT IS SMALL, YES YOU CAN.
LITTLE GIRL.
YOU SHOW GRANDMA HER ROOM OK I WILL HERE IT IS GRANDMA
WOW.
IT WAS PANTED YES MAMA IT WAS HOW DO YOU LIKE THE COLOR?

OK SON, AND THE ROOM IS REAL NICE LET'S GO OUTLET MAMA SETTLE IN.

I WILL BE OUT SOON. MAMA THERE IS SOME CLEAN TOWELS IN THERE FOR YOU IF YOU WANT.

TO TAKE A BATH, YES, I WILL GET CLEANUP MAMA IF YOU WANTED SOMETHING TO EAT.

LET US KNOW I WILL NOW WE WILL BE IN OUR ROOM IF YOU NEED US. I WILL BE FINE.
OK MAMA JOE WE HAD A BAD STORM HERE THE GOOD LORD KEEP US SAFE.
YES, I KNOW SAW IT ON THE NEWS I WANTED TO CALL YOU BUT I CHANGE MY MIND.

I PRAY INSTEAD I HAVE FAITH IN GOD ME TO SAID HIS WIFE; GOD IS SO GOOD.
WELL, I NEED TO MAKE SOME SUPPER WHAT DO YOU THINK YOUR MAMA WOULD LIKE.
SHE CAN EAT ANYTHING SHE LIKES VEGETABLES THE MOST.
OK I WILL MAKE HER WHAT SHE WANTS.

I THINK SHE IS TAKING A NAP AFTER HER BATH LETS LET HER REST. SHE NEEDS THAT.
SHE DROVE MOST OF THE WAY HERE SHE DID NOT WANT ME TO HELP HER.
HOW WAS YOUR FLIGHT IT WAS OK I WENT TO SLEEP? THAT IS THE FIRST TIME.
I HAVE FLEW IN A WHILE IT WAS NICE UP IN THE SKY. YES, I GUESS IT WAS.

BUT I DID MISS YOU ALL NOW IT IS TIME FOR ME TO WATCH A LITTLE BALL GAMES.

I MISS THAT MAMA HAS HER MOVES SHE WANTS TO WATCH SO I WATCH, WITH HER

IT SEEM LIKE THE TIME JUST STOOD STILL WHEN YOU LEFT, WE MISSED YOU SO MUCH.

AND THAT STORM SCARED US TO DEATH WE WENT INTO THE BASEMENT UNTIL IT WAS OVER. I DID CALL MRS ODELL SHE SAID THEY WERE ALL OK.

YOU WERE ON THE ROAD SO I COULD NOT CALL YOU IF IT GOT REAL
I KNOW BUT MAMA STOP AT THE STORE AND THERE TV WAS ON THE WEATHER.

SO JUST TOLD MAMA LETS PRAY MAMA SAID, YES, I KNOW JESUS WOULD. TAKE CARE OF YOU ALL I ALSO PRAY FOR THE ODELLS THAT IS SO GOOD.

SHE SAID SHE WOULD PRAY FOR YOU SO WE ALL ARE SAFE. JESUS TOOK CARE OF US.

SUPPER IS DONE GO TELL YOUR MAMA TO COME TO THE TABLE. SO, HE DID MAMA SUPPER IS DONE COME ON AND EAT, OK SON I AM COMING.
MAMA YOU SIT HERE BU CINDY OK SOMETHING MUST BE GOOD.

YES, MAMA RUTH MADE YOU SOME GOOD FOOD
WELL THAT BATH. SURE.
DID FEEL GOOD I FEEL ASLEEP AND YOU DID NOT
HAVE TO GO THOUGH
SO MUCH TROUBLE.


THIS IS REAL GOOD RUTH THANK YOU WHEN
ARE YOU ALL COMING TOMY.
PLACE I DO NOT KNOW MAMA.


ONE DAY MABY MAMA THEY ARE MOVING NOW
YES, I SEE THEY ARE. THEY ARE MOVING BACK TO
FLORIDA.
I WILL MISS THEM MAMA, BUT YOU DID NOT
KNOW THEM THAT WELL I KNOW.
MAMA BUT THEY WERE NICE TO ME.

WELL, THEY SAID THEY WOULD WRITE YOU AND
CALL YOU YES MAMA THEY DID,

SO, LOOK FOR A LETTER FROM THEM I WILL WILL
MAMA YOU CAN WATCH TV.
ARE DO WHAT YOU WANT TO DO GRANDMA I AM
GOING TO GO GET MY FRIEND SUE,

SHE KNOWS YOU WERE COMING I TOLD HER SHE
WANTS TO SEE YOU. CINDY, I BROUGHT.
YOU SOMETHING GO GET MY BAG OK GRANDMA
HERE LOOK I BOUGHT YOU.
AND YOUR FRIEND A DRESS THANKS GRANDMA.

I WILL GO SEE SUE TOMORROW BRING HER TO SEE YOU HERE IS SOME THING FOR YOU.
AND YOUR FRIEND TO PUT IN YOUR HAIR.

OK GRANDMA THANKS I WILL GO LAY DOWN, BUT IF YOU WANT ME TO HELP.
YOU I WILL NO MAMA I WILL DO IT. OK I WILL GET SOME REST.

GRANDMA GOODNIGHT SAID CINDY GOOD NIGHT YOU HAVE A NICE NIGHT

OK I WILL MAMA IS SO TIRED SAID MR. WHITE I KNOW SAY HIS WIFE.

THE NEXT MORNING IS SUNDAY MAMA WE ARE GOING TO CHURCH. WOULD YOU LIKE TO GO?
YOU MEAN THE CHURCH WHERE I USED TO GO YES MAMA SURE I WOULD.

LIKE TO SEE SOME OF MY OLD FRIENDS. IT HAS BEEN A WHILE DADDY COME HERE CAN YOU TELL ME GRANDMA NAME?
YOU DO NOT KNOW HER NAME? NO DADDY I CALL HER GRANDMA.

GRANDMA ARE YOU GOING TO CHURCH? WE GO TO YOUR CHURCH. YES, I DO.
OK I AM GOING TO WEAR THE DRESS YOU BROUGHT ME OK DEAR. NOW I WILL GET READY.

LOOK GRANDMA AT MY DRESS IT IS SO PRETTY. YES, IT IS CINDY. LOOK MAMA WHAT GRANDMA BROUGHT ME.

IT IS SO NICE.

YES, DEAR IT IS. I LIKE THE BLUE IT MATCH MY EYES GRANDMA MUST HAVE KNOW THAT.
I AM SURE SHE DID WILL I AM READY, OK MAMA WE ARE TO LET'S GO TO CHURCH.

OK AS THEY WERE GOING TO THE CHURCH LOOK CINDY, THAT IS WHERE YOUR GRANDPA AND ME LIVED.
WHEN HE PASS AWAY IS THAT WHY YOU MOVED SAID CINDY? YES, IT IS

I MISS HIM SO MUCH HE HAS BEEN GONE TO HEAVEN A LONG TIME .ONE DAY I WILL SEE HIM AGAIN.

YES, MAMA I MISS DADDY TO BUT WHY DON.T YOU MOVE BACK. YOU HAVE FRIENDS.
AND YOUR HOUSE IS STILL STANDING YOU LEFT ME WITH THE KEYS. NO ONE HAS LIVE THERE SINCE YOU LEFT.

YOU CANNOT GET AWAY FROM YOUR PAST NO ICAN.T SON. IT JUST I MISS YOUR FATHER SO MUCH.

WHY DON.T WE GO THERE AFTER I GET OFF WORK AND LET. YOU SEE THE OLD PLACE.
OK JOE, WE CAN DO THAT I HATE TO LEAVE YOUR BROTHER HE IS THE REASON I MOVE THERE.

DID YOU TELL HIM YOU WERE COMING HERE?
YES, I DID. HE HAD TO STAY.

WITH HIS WIFE JOYCE SHE WAS SICK I TOLD HIM I WOULD NOT BE GONE.
LONG HE DID NOT LIKE THAT I HAVE LIVE THERE SINCE YOUR DAD PASS AWAY.

IT HAS BEEN OVER FOUR YEARS NOW IF I MOVE BACK IT WILL JUST. KILLED HIM.
BUT I WANT TO SEE THE OLD HOME PLACE ME TO MAMA YOUR DADDY HAS BEEN SICK LONG TIME.

YES MAMA, I KNOW YOU TOLD ME SO MANY TIMES I REMEMBER HIM GOING.
HE HAS BEEN ON MY MIND TO WILL HERE WE ARE AT YOUR OLD CHURCH.

LET'S GET OUT THE PASTOR IS THERE WELCOME IN THE PEOPLE. PASTOR GREEN.
MRS WHITE, SO GLAD TO SEE YOU. ARE YOU HERE TO STAY NO JUST VISIT MY SON AND FAMILY?
WELL WELCOME LINDA I AM SURE YOU HAVE LOTS OF FRIENDS HERE.
COME ON IN EVERYONE.
THE LADIES COME TO SEE MRS WHITE HELLO MRS ROBERTS SO GOOD TO SEE YOU.

YOU TO MRS WHITE ARE YOU BACK TO LIVE NO JUST VIST MY SON AND FAMILY.
WE SURE HAVE MISS YOU.

WE IT IS TIME TO START THE SERVICE. WE HAVE A SPECIAL GUEST IN OUR SERVICE MRS LINDA WHITE SHE MOVE OFF NOW SHE IS WITH US

STAND UP MRS WHITE, GIVE HER SOME LOVE GOD BLESS YOU.
SO GLAD TO SEE YOU NOW LET'S SING AND HAVE A GOOD TIME IN THE LORD.
WILL THE SERVICE IS OVERTIME TO GO HOME?
IT WAS LIKE OLD TIMES; SON YES MAMA IT WAS I REMEMBER WHEN YOU.
BROUGHT ME HERE AS A CHILD.


I GUESS YOU DO IT HAS BEEN MANY YEARS FORTY-FIVE YES, WE HAD. A BIRTHDAY PARTY.
FOR HIM LAST WEEK OCTOBER THE TWENTY YES MAMA I THOUGHT. ABOUT YOU.

BUT I JUST COULD NOT CALL BECAUSE IT WAS SO PAIN FULL SORRY MAMA.
YES, DEAR SHE BEGAN TO CRY MAMA IT WILL BE OK YOU WILL.
SEE DADDY ONE DAY. YES, I KEEP ON TELLING MYSELF THAT.
BUT IT HAS BEEN SO LONELY. GRANDMA GRANDPA IS WAITING ON YOU TO.


HE HAS WROTE YOU A SONG LET ME SING TO YOU. OK DEAR HERE IS HIS.
WORDS I WILL WAIT FOR YOU IF I LEAVE BEFORE YOU DO. I KNOW

THAT IT HAS BEEN SO LONG BUT I STILL SEE YOUR EYES OF BLUE THE SMILE.
ON YOUR PRETTY FACE IS WHAT I REMEMBER OF YOU DO NOT.
FORGET OUR GOOD TIMES TOGETHER I WILL WAIT FOR YOU GRANDMA
I FOUND THIS WITH GRANPA NAME FOR YOU.
WHERE WAS IT DEAR? ON YOUR DRESSER I HAVE IT AT HOME I REMEMBER SOME OF IT.
I WANTED TO GIVE IT TO YOU, BUT I DID NOT WANT TO SEE YOU CRY.


THANK YOU DEAR WHEN DID YOU FIND IT? DADDY CARRIED ME THERE.
I PICK IT UP SO YOU HAVE HAD IT ALL THIS TIME? YES, I HAVE.

WHY DID I NOT SEE IT I WONDER, MAMA, YOU WERE SO UPSET THAT IS WHY.
YOU DID NOT KNOW NO MAMA SHE DID NOT SHOW IT TO ME.?


WILL THAT IS JUST LIKE YOUR DADDY WHEN WE WERE GOING TO GATHER.
HE SAYED POMES TO ME AND SONG SONGS TO ME. HE WAS JUST SUCH.
A GOOD PERSON.


I KNOW MAMA I HEARD HIM SINGING TO YOU HE LOVE YOU SO MUCH. AND HE WANTED TO MAKE YOU HAPPY.

YES, SON, HE WAS A GOOD MAN AND I LOVE HIM TO BUT I HAVE GOT TO GO ON WITH MY LIFE.

I CAN NOT KEEP ON LIVING THE PAST. HE WOULD TELL ME TO GO ON AND BE HAPPY.
SO THAT IS WHAT I AM GOING TO DO. I AM MOVING BACK GRANDMA I AM GLAD YOU SAID THAT WE ARE HOME I HAVE SOMETHING ELSE TO SHOW YOU.
OK LETS ALL GO INSIDE,

HERE GRANDMA LOOK WHAT I FOUND THE SAME DAY I PICK UP THE SONG.
LISTEN JOE THIS IS WHAT YOUR DADDY WROTE LINDA BY THE TIME YOU READ THIS; I WILL BE GONE TO HEAVEN NOW I KNOW YOU WILL WANT TO MOVE TO FLORIDA DON'T STAY IN OUR PLACE BECAUSE.

I BOUGHT IT FOR YOU AND OUR KIDS.
JUST STAY THERE AND KEEP ON GOING TO CHURCH UNTIL WE MEET AGAIN.
I WILL WAIT FOR YOU YOUR LOVING HUSBAND JACK

SO, DADDY WANTED YOU TO STAY HERE I GUESS SO HE NEVER SAID SO
BUT THE LETTER SAID IT THE TEARS WERE IN HER EYES AS SHE WENT TO HER ROOM.
MAMA ARE YOU OK YES SO; I AM OK JUST A LITTLE UPSET

I DID NOT KNOW HE FELT THAT WAY SON WILL YOU HELP ME MOVE BACK.?

YES, MAMA I WILL I KNOW YOUR BROTHER WANT LIKE IT BUT I WANT TO DO.
YOUR FATHER WELL.

OK MAMA WE WILL DO THAT I NEED TO GO BACK SO I CAN GET EVERYTHING.
STARTED GET MY BILLS PAID AND EVERYTHING TURN OFF THAN. I WILL MOVE BACK.

I WILL STAY HERE TILL TUESDAY AND THEN I NEED TO GO BACK.
DO YOU WANT ME TO GO WITH YOU?
NO, I WILL BE OK JOE I HAVE GOT TO CARRY OUT YOUR DADDYS. WISHES.

THAT IS WHAT HE WANTS I WILL DO I WILL HAVE MY THINGS SHIPPED HERE.
LET'S GO TO THE HOUSE NOW OK MAMA IF THAT IS WHAT YOU WANT.
YES, THAT IS WHAT I WANT.

IT HAS BEEN SOME TIME SINCE I HAVE BEEN THERE OK LETS LOAD UP. AND GO.
IT IS NOT THAT FOR FROM HERE AS THEY ARE RIDING YOU KNOW MAMA.
SAID MRS WHITE I WAS WONDER WHY I HAVE SUCH A GOOD HUSBAND NOW I KNOW WHY,


HIS DADDY WAS SO GOOD TO YOU YES DEAR HE TAKE AFTER HIS DADDY.
I NOTICE THAT WHEN HE WAS VERY YOUNG, HE WAS SUCH A GOOD KID

NOW WE ARE HERE MAMA SON COULD I HAVE FEW MINUTES INSIDE BEFORE.
YOU ALL COME IN YES MAMA. WE WILL WAIT FOR YOU AS HIS MAMA
WALK UPON THE PORCH SHE BEGAIN TO TRIMBLE. SHE WALK INTO HER HOUSE WILL IT IS LIKE I LEFT IT


I WILL HAVE TO CLEAN IT BEFORE I MOVE IN IT YOU ALL CAN COME IN.
OK MAMA LOOK HERE IS ONE OF YOUR DADDY COAT SON WHY.
DON.T YOU TAKE IT. I NEVER GAVE HIS CLOTHES AWAY. HE HAD SOME.
NICE CLOTHES I HAVE GOT TO GIVE THEM TO SOMEONE


AND THERE IS LOTS OF WORK NEEDS TO BE DONE SHE BEGAN TO CRY CINDY SHOW GRANDMA WHERE YOU FOUND.
THAT RIGHT HERE GRANDMA HERE IS HIS WALLET THERE.
IS MONEY INSIDE HERE COUNT IT MAMA THERE IS AROUND FIVE THOUSAND DOLLARS HERE.


HE NEVER WANTED TO PUT HIS MONEY IN THE BANK.
MAMA THEY IS MORE THERE IS ANOTHER TEN THOUSAND HERE. WOW HE NEVER TOLD ME HE HAD MONEY.

I GUESS HE PUT IT THERE FOR ME. YES MAMA I GUESS SO.
WILL I CAN USED IT TO MOVE HERE SON YOU TAKE THE FIVE AND. I WILL KEEP THE TEN ARE YOU SURE MAMA?
YES, YOU NEED IT FOR YOUR FAMILY THANKS MAMA, I KNOW. YOUR DADDY WOULD WANT THAT.

SO NOW THAT I HAVE SAW THEIR HOUSE, LETS GO MAMA DO YOU WANT THE? KEY
NO, YOU HOLD ON TO IT IN CASE YOU NEED IT WHEN I GO TO BE WITH YOUR DADDY. THE HOUSE GOES TO YOU. MAMA WHAT ABOUT TONY YOU LET ME TAKE CARE OF? THAT.

I DO NOT WANT TONY TO HAVE IT BECAUSE IT WILL LOOSE IT GAMBLING. MAMA.
I DID NOT KNOW THAT. YES, HE HAS CHANGE HE IS NOT THE SAME. I HAVE GIVE HIM SO MUCH MONEY HE LOOSE IT SO I AM TIRED•
I WILL NOT GIVE HIM ANOTHER PENNY.

SORRY MAMA THAT IS ONE REASON I AM MOVING BACK. I DID NOT WANT TO TELL YOU.
ABOUT YOUR BROTHER BUT YOU WILL FIND OUT WHEN HE CALLS YOU ASKING. FOR MONEY, MAMA, HE ALREADY HAS BEFORE YOU CAME HERE HE SAID HE LOST HIS JOB. AND NEED MONEY FOR BILLS AND GROCERS. WHAT DID YOU SAY?
I TOLD HIM I DID NOT HAVE ANY MONEY. HE GOT MAD AND HUNG UP ON ME,

THAT IS MY LITTLE TONY. HE THINK IF HIS SELF BEFORE ANYONE ELSE .SO HE DID NOT TELL. YOU MAMA.
NO SON HE DID NOT.

WILL MAMA I SURE WISH I COULD DO SOMETHING SO YOU HAVE A FAMILY.
TONY HAS A FAMILY HE DOES NOT CARE ABOUT YOU CANNOT HELP, ANYONE THAT WANT TO HELP HIS SELF.
YOUR DADDY SAID THE SAME THING.

HE WORK AND WE HAVE THAT HOUSE AND OTHER THINGS TO PROVE. IT.
BUT TONY DOES NOT WANT TO WORK. SON I JUST PRAY FOR YOUR BROTHER. THAT IS ALL I CAN DO.

WILL MAMA LETS GO TO BED TOMORROW IS ANOTHER DAY. YES, SON IT IS.
GOODNIGHT MAMA GOODNIGHT SON SEE YOU IN THE MORNING.
I WILL GO TO WORK. BUT I WILL SEE YOU WHEN I GET IN .IN THE BED ROOM MAMA IS NOT THINKING ABOUT DADDY IT IS TONY.
SHE WORRY ABOUT SHE HAS BEEN SUPPORT HIM FOR A LONG TIME.

SHE HAS YES BUT SHE HAS MADE UP HER MIND TO MOVE BACK. HERE.
THAT IS GOOD. ARE YOU GOING TO PUT THE MONEY IN THE BANK?
BUT YOU DO IT FOR ME.

I HAVE GOT TO GO TO WORK HERE IT IS. PUT SOME IN TO OUR SAVINGS OK I WILL DON. YOU WANT TO HAVE SOME IN YOUR POCKET?

NO, I STILL HAVE SOME OUT OF THE TRIP I DID NOT USED IT ALL. MAMA PAYED FOR EVERYTHING. SHE WAS SO GLADE TO SEE ME WE ATE OUT IN THE PLACE SHE. GOES TO.

OK I WILL PUT IT IN OUR ACCOUNT TOMORROW NOW I NEED. TO.
GO TO SLEEP WORK TOMORROW ME TO SO THE NEXT MORNING. THEY GOT UP.;
CINDY DADDY WENT TO WORK. GRANDMA ARE YOU UP? NO NOT YET.
I WILL BE UP SOON.

I AM GOING OVER TO GET MY FRIEND SUE SHE WANTS TO SEE YOU. OK DEAR.
I WILL HAVE A CUP OF COFFEE MAMA HERE IS YOUR COFFEE. WOW IT IS GOOD.
DO YOU WANT ANY BREAKFAST NO JUST COFFEE? I WILL EAT LATER; ON TODAY.
MAMA DID YOU GET A GOOD NIGHT SLEEP? YES, DEAR THAT BED WAS REAL NICE.

OK, WHAT DO YOU WANT TO DO TODAY I AM JUST GOING TO REST. THAT IS ALL.
I WANT TO DO I HAVE NEVER BEEN SO TIRED SINCE I PICK COTTON AND.
THAT HAS BEEN A LONG TIME.

WHEN DOES JOE GET OFF WORK HE WILL BE HOME AROUND FIVE HE GETS OFF AROUND FOUR-THIRTY.
HE IS SO TIRED WHEN HE GETS IN ALL HE WANTS IS A BATH AND WATCH.
THE TV. HE LIKE TO GO FISHING WHEN HE WAS A LITTLE. BOY. HE WENT WITH HIS DADDY.

HE LIKE THAT AND MY HUSBAND WANTED HIM TO GO WITH HIM. SO, THEY WOULD LEAVE EARLY. AND THAT WAS ALL THEY TALK ABOUT WHEN THEY GOT HOME. DOES JOE EVER SAY ANYTHING ABOUT FISHING? NO BUT FOR.
HIS BIRTHDAY I BOUGHT HIM A POLE HE LIKE SO MUCH,

IF I SAY SOMETHING ABOUT HIM AND HIS DAD GOING FISHING, HE WOULD LET LOOSE ON WHAT HE AND HIS DAD DID.
I WILL SAY SOMETHING ABOUT IT WHEN HE GETS HOME. HE REALLY LIKE FISHING. WITH HIS DADDY.
ONE NIGHT IT WAS LIKE A SONG I LIKE NEVER GET HIM TO STOP.
HE JUST WOULD NOT FORGET IT, I GUESS BECAUSE HE WAS WITH HIS DADDY. THAT IS WHY HE MISSING HIM SO .

HE IS HERE MAMA WAIT TILL HE COMES IN YOU WILL SEE.

HA MAMA HOW WAS YOUR DAY?

OK SON, CAN I ASK YOU SOMETHING WHAT MAMA YOU REMEMBER GOING FISHING? WITH YOUR DADDY.
DO I EVERY WE HAD SOME GOOD TIMES DADDY AND ME.
I WOULD GET THE LINES READY WHILE DADDY GET EVERYTHING OUT OF THE TRUCK
.ONE DAY WE GOT STUCK AND WE LIKE TO HAVE NEVER GOT OUT IT WAS SO MUDDY

DADDY WAS SO MAD.
BUT FINALLY, A MAN CAME BY AND HELP US OUT.

IT WAS SO FUNNY TO ME WE ROCK THAT OLD TRUCH BACK AND FORWARD TILL WE GOT IT OUT.

# BOOK I

The story that I am about to tell you started in the fifties; where two little girls became friends; they were different colors; Sue was black and Cindy was white; but they did not care what anyone said to them' they still played with each other; they like to play with dolls; and Sue would go to Cindy home; and spend the night she did not care they were close friends. one day they went up town with there mother., shopping Cindy mother said you two stay here in the park; while we go to the grocers store. and I well bring you a bar of candy. you can watch out for each other; we well be back soon; ok mother said Sue we well be ok so Cindy and Sue sat on the bench; Cindy went to the bath room you stay here

Sue; ok yes, I well be ok so she left at that minute a man came by you are not supposed to sat on that bench get up and go home girl Sue look up at the man with a tear in her eye. About that time Cindy came out what did he say to you? she put her arms around Sue it is ok I well ask mother why;

The two women walk out of the store; Cindy ran to her mother; ha what is wrong? Mother Sue and me were setting on the beach this man came by he asked sue not to sat on it told her to leave mother why? Honey I cannot tell you why. not now. you are to little to know what I am talking about; maybe when you get older. but mother it is not fair for him to tell her to leave. what is the difference between sue and me? just colors that is it God made us right mother yes Cindy you are right? well we well be friends for ever Sue was real upset she ran into the street a car hit her.

Sue mother ran after her please don't let my baby die. Cindy was standing by her. Please don't die Sue I am her with you. You are going to be all right Cindy began to cry. Her mother call the ambulance Cindy was by her side giving her support all the way to the hospital;

Sue mom brought Cindy home; for many weeks Sue stay in the hospital; Cindy prayed for her one and only friend; she said please God let SUE be ok; I well be a good girl. Cindy visit Sue as much as she could. bringing her things. to make her feel better. she sure did miss her sometimes she would cry she was having dinner one day dad why can. t Sue and me play with each other? God did not make a mistake did he father? With Sue black and me white why was that father? she is my best friend she is hurt no God did not make a mistake reply the father;

He knew what he was doing; reply the father. I cannot explain what I am trying to say. you are to young to understand Cindy said that is what mother said. I do not get any answer. I well find out another way. I promised Sue I would. what the man said upset her. father I am going over to Sue house ok? Now Cindy don. t go bother Sue mom she well tell you the same. when Cindy got to Sue house, she saw Mrs. Odell standing on the porch hi Cindy how are you. good but I have something I need to talk to you about. do you have time? sure what is on your mind? I just left my father I wonted to know why Sue and me cannot play with each other. do you know why? honey I wish I could tell you. But I can. t you would not understand well that is what I thought. reply Cindy.

Oh, by the way how is Sue doing? She is better I wanted to go see her tonight to give her some good news. what is that dear? She wanted me to find out why we can't play with each other? I can tell you this God said there would be war between the nation. this could be your answer. you well understand more when you get older. that is what everyone is saying. I cannot get a straight answer; don. t you think you and Sue are to young to asked them kind of question? Why don. t you pray about it? you mean like I do at night? When I am down on my knees? Yes, that is right ok I well I think I can get more out of God than anyone else; maybe so

Mrs. Odell when Sue gets out we are going to play with each other; I do not care what any one says;. no one can brake friends up that is right reply Sue mom.

We do have good times together we play dolls and games. Mrs. Odell, we do not have anyone else I know honey; you two have been friends forever; yes, you are right and you mom and me have been friends now I guess I well go home *so* I can get ready go see my friend. so, Cindy left when she got home her mother was there. how is Sue doing you did go see did you? yes mother she is better mother I miss sue I am going to see her tonight. may I mother.? Could you drive me? Reply Cindy sure after supper. Cindy got ready while her mother finished supper. come on and eat said her mother. I well be there as soon as I comb my hair. Sue was setting up in bed hi Cindy said Sue. I am so glad to see you;

Cindy went over to Sue bed, I have missed you *so* much, how are you doing? said Cindy good thanks for asking is your mom coming to see you tonight? No she will be here in the morning. the doctor is sending me home soon,. I will be so glad said Cindy. I am so sorry about your accident will they did give me lots of ice cream it was good, now you will be going home and that makes me happy, in 2 weeks Sue got out of the hospital, Cindy went with her mom to pick her up, she still had to take it easy, doctors' orders

Cindy was at Sue house, doing things for her. every day. one day Cindy said to her mother, I want to buy Sue something a get well present ok, Cindy I well take you shopping this week end.

Mother I know Sue will like what I get her, Mother I ask you a something you never answer it, what are you talking about Cindy? Mother about why Sue and me cannot play together, why mother? Cindy I cannot answer that, why mother? Because there is no answer, ok mother, mother I am going to bed, I think Sue is doing better thank God, I will go back to School tomorrow, ok Cindy said her mother, you have a good night, do not forget to brush your teeth, and say your pray, I will mother, the next morning her mother call ·her, are you up Cindy? Cindy did not answer, Cindy are you up? I need to know what you want fur breakfast? I will skip breakfast mother, I need to call Sue ask her if she is going to the movies tonight, you need to eat said her mother.

Never mind Cindy, you know Sue why don. t you spend the night with me. will I need to ask mother, you can call her from my phone, ok I will but I still need to get some clothes, you can wear some of my clothes, you have been wearing them for a while and I have help myself to yours, ok Sue call her mother, hello ha Sue what are you calling for I though you would be home by now, mom Cindy wants me to spend the night, honey you need to come home and get you *some* clothes, no I don't. t mom I well wear some of my friends Cindy. you sure that is what you want? yes mom I see you tomorrow after school. ok honey love you you to mom, ok Cindy mom said it was ok. will then let's go tell mom, mom Sue is spending the night. with me, ok good show her where you will sleep, what do you want to do, will it is early we can watch TV for its black and white, the night went by with the two girls eating chicken and ice cream the next morning.

The next thing Cindy heard was her mother calling her name, get up Cindy get ready for school, ask Sue what she wants for breakfast, Sue are you awake? Sue move her head to the side, I cannot belive it is morning, you girls must stay up late last night said Cindy mom, a little late we both went to sleep watching

Lucy she is so funny, she is said Sue, Sue I am going to get my bath, you can go with mom and she well show you where to set to eat breakfast, I will be out In a little, I am not to hungry will if you want to stay in bed, we can eat together, it is up to you, I will stay in bed, when Cindy got in to the tub, *she* turn on the water, oh no I left my Robe on the bed, Sue yes could you please get my Robe on the bed?, and bring it to me, sure I will. she laugh here it is thanks Sue anything else? no I well be out In a little, I change my mind I will go to the kitchen and have some toast and milk. said Sue.

When Sue went to the kitchen Cindy mom was eating her breakfast Sue did you sleep ok? Yes, I did thanks for asking, what do you want for breakfast? I think I will take some toast and a glass of milk; can you get the bread is in the bread box? And you can toast it the butter is to the right there on the table, thank you Mrs. white, by the way where is Cindy at? she is going to be late for school, she is still taken her bath, here she is mom I am running late, Sue are you ready? yes, I am I need to go by the house and get my books, ok we better leave now bye mom bye Mrs. white, bye girls.

Mom I well be late if I do not go now, it was nice to have you spend the night, thank you Mrs. white, when the girls got to Sue house, I well see you after school Sue, ok Cindy, Cindy and Sue had found some money Cindy has this on her mind, they did not want to tell anyone about it, the day pass by real fast, Cindy went to Sue house, when she knock at the door, Mrs. Odell answer hi

Cindy how are you doing, fine is Sue home yet? she is in her room I will go get her, she has been upset, I do not know what is wrong, Sue Cindy is here, mother tell her I will be out in a littlee., Cindy come on in she will be out soon.

Hi Cindy how are you.? I am ok what about you, Cindy I have something to tell you, Sue what is it? Cindy you know I have a boyfriend? This boy Tom yes will I love him. I think he loves me, but I did something wrong what;' I sleep with him, and now I think I am PG oh know have you missed a period? yes a couple, what are you going to do? have you thought about telling your mother and dad? ho no I cannot., that would upset them. my mother and dad would not understand, it would kill them, the reason I told you we are best friends, Sue have you told Tom? no I cannot, why not? because he is still young and I do not know how he would take it.

You must tell him, you will know how he feels, will; you tell him for me? no sue that is for you to do; I do not know him; and he would tell me it was not anything to me; what about your boyfriend could he tell him, as Cindy put her arms around Sue, we will do something, I think you should tell your mom, she could help you, Sue I have got to go, we will talk about this later, don't do anything until we con our talk, as Cindy hug *Sue* neck. see you later, when you feel better call me, as Cindy left, she pet Sue dog. good boy, Sue I think he is hungry he is I guess.

When Cindy left Mrs. Odell came back into the living room, she left fast said Sue mom,; Yes she did she had things to do, I think she had a date tonight, when Cindy arrived home, her mom was there, you sound like you are tired?, well I did run a ways, The doorbell rings, Cindy can you answer the door? when Cindy open the door there stood a old man dress in a blue suite, I hope I have the right address, are you Cindy white? yes I am who may you be. my name is frank smith, oh I know who you are, you are the one that lost the money and diamonds that my friend and me found, please to meet you, you to young lady, is your friend here? no but I can call her, she does not live for from here, come on in set down, this is my mom, Mrs. white, mom this is Mr. smith he come here to give Sue and me a reward, for finding the money and diamonds remember I told you and dad? yes welcome to our home Mr. smith, I will call Sue she will be here soon that is very nice of you to come and thank the girls.

I call Sue she is on her way over, yes I am glad you have her to come over, the news people are coming, *so* you and your friend will be on the news, so I can give you the check, I want you to have, it, was *so* nice of you all to turn it in, Sue will like that, she should have been here before now I will call again hello Mrs. Odell this is Cindy is Sue still there? honey I forgot to tell her here she is, hi Cindy what is up Sue Mr. Smith is here you know the one that the money belongs too we found,? Yes, I remember will he wants to meet you and we are going to be on the news so hurry get over here, I am leaving now, mom I am going over to Cindy the money we found the person that it belongs to is at Cindy, he wants to meet me ok you hurry I will be back soon. in a little Sue knock on Cindy door come on in said Cindy Sue I won't you to meet Mr. Smith.

Please to meet you Sue, the news men are coming in behind Sue where do we set up said the news men to Cindy mom? You all can put it in our living room, when they got everything set up, Mr. Smith you and the girls set here, Mr. Smith how did you loose your money? Tell the views how you felt when you lost your money, and you could not find it, I look everywhere I had my wife to call her friends ask them to go look for it, I could nor sleep that night I call the police and that is when I found it, at the station, they told me two young ladies turn it in I was so happy, you have a big reward for these girls yes, I do, as we understand it two hundred thousand dollars, yes that is right.

Ok your name is Cindy? yes sir; and you are Sue? with the pretty blue dress on. Yes sir, I need to know how you feel since the owner has come forward? we will start with Cindy, first, did you think the police would find the owner "?, maybe I did not know I am glad they did. you was the one to find all of the money and diamond. s? yes, I was and you want your friend to have some of it? Yes sir, how do you feel about that Sue? well we are best friends we have know each other a long time. we all wish you the best what will you to get with your money? Will Mr. Smith you can give the girls the check now.

As Mr. Smith gives Cindy the money, you two do not spend this all-in-one place, everyone this is channel 8 news, you can see what happen when you are honest person, like these two girls its nice to know you people, as Mr. Smith leaves, the girls began to jump up and down, we are rich., said Sue; not really said Cindy, … we do have lots of money, Sue did you talk to your mom yet? No, I have not, I do not want to upset mom, then what are you going to do? if you are pregnant? I do not know, why don. t you call Tom? talk to him, about that time in walks Cindy mom, what are you to talking about? Cindy looked at Sue, Sue do you care if I tell mom? She may know what to do, tell me what; are you in trouble Sue?

Yes, I am in real bad trouble, what is it child? Sue put her head down, go ahead Sue tell my mom., Mrs. White do you promised not to tell my mom? Yes, I well promised, ok you feel real bad about what you are going to tell me Sue? Yes, I do, Sue ran out the door, Sue come back said Cindy, yes come back reply Cindy mom, Sue stops she turn around, ok I will tell you, Cindy will you tell your mom first? Mom Sue thinks she is pregnant what. How did this happen? Mom she did not mean for it to happen. What are you going to do Sue? Mom I thought you could help her, I do not know how I can help her, why can't she tell her mom, mom if that was me what would you do, you are right Cindy may she should wait, before she tells her mom.

Have you thought about telling Tom your boyfriend? mom do you think that is wise? well Cindy after all he is responsible maybe he will tell you what to do, why don. t you tell him, to meet you here, at our place, and we all can tell him, would you do that for me Mrs. white? yes, honey I will help you any way I can, do you know his number? you can used my phone, Cindy I need to talk to you in the bath room, mom Sue wants me to follow her to the bathroom. she has something to tell me, ok but hurry, Cindy what I did not tell you is Tom he is white, there you go again why can't you go with your on kind? you are asking for trouble, it is ok Cindy saw a tear fall from Sue eyes, I thought you would understand, Sue does he know you are black, " look white to me but you are not, and when he finds out, let's go tell mom, maybe she has a answer, mom we have something to tell you, ok what is it? mom what Sue did not *tell* us her friend is white, you have got to be kidding, Sue why? I look white and I thought I could fool him in thinking I was, never mind about that, you call him we need to get the truth out and this is the only way to do it, let's see what Tom says, Sue called Tom, hi Tom hi sweetheart what is wrong? I need to talk to you., what is wrong, I cannot tell you over the phone, but Mrs. white well tell you how to get here, this is where my friend lives Cindy.

I will be there real soon, mom did Sue boyfriend sound nice? yes, he did, good maybe he will not be to mad when he finds out she told him a lie well that is a change she has got to face, where did Sue go mom? she went home while you were in your room but she will be back soon, I sure hope she gets back before Tom gets here, here she comes now I see her walking toward the house, Tom well be here soon where did you go? I had something to do., you need to get ready to face him, I hope your mom helps *me*, we well.

Cindy will you get some chips and some cokes? Put them on the table, he may want something to eat, and drink, Sue do you want to help me? Sure Cindy, I need to do something to keep my mind off of things, you put the plates on the table, and I well get the chips and cokes, mom someone is at the door, Cindy puts her arms around Sue it is ok, Mrs. white answer the door hi you must be Tom, Sue ran to Tom she put her arms around him, Mrs. white almost lost her bounce, Tom this is my friend mom and here is my friend Cindy, Mrs. white I would like for you to meet Tom my boyfriend, nice to meet you both reply Tom, come on in and set down we have some chips and coke, would you like some said Mrs. white? sure I guess so, I well eat some while we talk, I have some cake to if you want any.

Sure, that will be nice, I made some ham salad sandwich too Tom if you would like some? you all thought I was hungry why was I called here not to eat I hope, no I just wanted to be nice to my daughter friend boyfriend said Mrs. white. Tom Sue has something to tell you, what is it honey? don't be mad at me but I may be pregnant, what yes, I have know this for two months, Sue you don't know this for sure? No, I don't but it is a change I might be, Sue have you told your mom are dad? no I have not, will we have got to tell them, you mean you will face mom and dad with this? You want mind? No, I do not mind, we could get married, no we cannot I am to young, I need to finished School, and I know that well be what my mom and dad well want, Mrs. white the food is real good thank you, eat as much as you want.

Tom what do you think about Sue if she is pregnant said Cindy? will if she is, we will see what happen when she finds out, I willl not leave her like some guys would do I love Sue, Tom could you come into the living room with me I would like to speak to you without the girls listen, ok Mrs. white? Girls we well be back in a little I want to ask Tom something, what do you want Mrs. white? Tom, I did not know you were white, what are you saying? I am saying Sue is black, did you know this? yes, I did she told me but it does not matter I love her., and I do not care what color she is, does your mom and dad know no? no but I do not think they are prejudice.

And in way I would not mind telling them, that is if Sue is pregnant, I well take her to the doctor, and then I will know, will at least we got that clear up, said Mrs. white, good to talk to you Tom, thank you Mrs. white, I am so glad Sue has you all for a friend, what were you all talking about said Sue? oh nothing said Mrs. white, Tom are you going to eat your cake? No Mrs. white I ate to much. if you all will excuse me, I have got to go, Sue I well call you later, ok Tom, Sue said as she kiss him on his lips, see you all later, glad to meet you all, and do not worry everything well work out, when Mrs. white close the door what a nice man, where did you meet him at Sue we were at the store I drop something he pick it up.

When did you tell him you were black? a few days after we started going together, what did he say? nothing much I think he was in shock, at first, but he got over it, now he is ok, I see said Mrs. white, he told me you told him, you must have forgot to tell Cindy, yes Sue I am your best friend did you over look that I am sorry Cindy it just never came up, so that was what you and Tom were talking about Mrs. white, yes that is one thing we were talking about, what did he tell you that you? had told him that is all, he also wants you to go be check, and that he would go with you, now that is what you call a good man, and they only come a dame a dozen.

He want to tell your mom and dad, I think he is going to call see if he can talk to them, so I think you should go tell them before he does, how do you think you mom is going to answer him as a white boy? I do not know do you think I should tell them tonight? Will I would before Tom brake the news, ok do you want me to go with you? No I need to do this myself, can I used your phone I want to see if dad make it home, first I want to talk to mom, before I talk to dad.

Sue calls her mom, yes Sue what is it? Mom is dad home? No honey he has not made it home yet, why? I will be home in a little while, I am over at my friends Cindy, I have something to tell you., are you ok yes mom I just need to tell you something, I will tell you when I get there, Sue hung the phone up, Cindy I am going home now, I well see you tomorrow don't forget call me after you talk to your mom, ok I will said Sue, as she left, mom do you think Sue will be ok? Sure, honey she will be find her mom will understand, she told you she would call, and I think she well, mom if this was me what would you do? I do not know mom I feel sorry for Sue, I knew it was something she wanted to talk about.

When Sue return home her dog bingo met her at the gate, hi bingo I am home she pet her dog, her mom was on the porch, honey what is wrong, Mom lets go in the house, when they got inside Sue look at her mom, now don't bring on the waterworks, I am here it cannot be that bad, yes it is mom, it is real bad, come here to your mom and tell me we can talk about it, ok mom. I think I am pregnant, how could this happen, mom this boy his name is Tom, we did not mean for it to happen, we love each other, love honey you a just a baby, have you told him? Yes, mom what does he want to do about it? Mom he wants to marry me, but you are to young.

That is what I told him he just wants to do the right thing, mom are you going to tell dad? Honey I need to tell him. He will find out soon, mom please don't tell him, not now, we will later., Sue what kind of background does this boy have? Does he go to church? His parents do you know them? Mom I did not tell you everything ok tell me, he is white, what; honey why would you date a white boy? We like each other, when we met, he is very good to me, we do not look at color, but honey what about the baby? What if it is white are you telling me that he knows you are black, ok young lady but you must know that there will come a time when you will have to.

Mom I need to take my shower, and afterwards I well call Cindy, I want her to know that we talk about Tom and everything is ok except I well need to tell my dad, honey I have got to make dinner, before your dad gets home from work, the phone is ringing I well get that, you hurry and get your shower, Sue mom answer the phone hello, my name is Tom Sue is my girlfriend is this her mom? Yes this is Mrs. Odall can I help you, yes my daughter is home she want to tell me about you, I am sorry I did not call you before she told you, so this is what you are calling me about? Yes, you are right. I want to meet you all sooner but I go to School I never could find the time, until now I hope this don't make you feel like I do not care, because I do very much., will what are you going to do about the *mess* you and Sue have got yourself into, Sue is to young to think of marriage and I do not know what her dad is going to say about this, are you going to tell him Mrs. Odell?

Yes, later I well need to tell him, I did promised Sue I would keep it to myself for a while, I plain on keeping that promised her dad may not want to hear this like I did she is his little girl and they are a bond between them, because she is our only child, Mrs.

Odell could I speak to Sue? Sue is taken her shower, she can call you later, does she have your number? yes tell her to call me, I have got to go thank you Mrs. Odell, when Sue finished her shower, mom who-was that on the phone? it was your friend Tom, what did he want? He wants you to call him, I well later, I have got to call Cindy before dad gets home, the phone is ringing hello Cindy yes Sue did you talk to your mom? Yes, we did.

Cindy hold on my dad just came home, mom has not told him yet, what did your mom say Cindy? she was very understanding I think, it was a shock to her dad and her are catholic you know what that is to them they do not believe in sex before marriage dad will have to think before he can deal with it, listen Cindy I have got to go, I will see you tomorrow, tell your mom I said thanks, she was very nice to me, ok Sue love you girl you to sayed Sue, mom that was Sue, she talk to her mom, now she knows everything, her dad came in while we were talking she had to go. is she telling her dad? later she will, mom I do not know what I would do if that were me.

I don't know what your dad would do, mom Sue dad they have not told him yet, you said that early today, the phone is ringing Cindy would you answer that? hello hello Cindy, yes, it is me, what is wrong Sue? Cindy you well not believe this what? Tom is on his way over to my house, he wants to talk to mom and dad, is your dad home now? no he went to the store, Cindy I don't know what to do, you know he wants to tell dad, Cindy dad is home I need to hung up so bye we well talk later, ok Sue call me later, after Sue hung up Sue I need to see you in my room said her mom.

Mom what do you want me for? we have got to tell your dad, ok honey? I well try before dad gets here, let's do it now mom he is in the kitchen, I have something to do first, hurry we well tell dad together, Bob Sue and me have something to tell you, but you have got to promised me you well not get mad? Sue come on we are waiting, I am coming, what is it tell me? Bob, we think Sue is pregnant, what '. we do not know for sure; we need to take her to the doctor have her checked, who does it belong to? do I know him? Sue dad I am sorry, a tear falls from her dad eyes, why, you could have come to us, her boyfriend is on his way, you knew this before me? no and yes Sue told me today, honey she was scared she did not want to tell me, I have something else to tell you., he is white what; Sue why dad I love him and he loves me, so that is supposed to settle everything, what about the baby? this is going a long ways said Sue dad.

Did Sue tell you this? Yes but he came by and we talked he is such a nice young man, I think you will like him, but what about Sue? if she is pregnant? what will we do she needs to finished School, and she is so young, will let's see what happened, I well take her to the doctor, tomorrow, mom someone is at the door, I will answer it, Bob that young man is here, now you be nice to him, ok I well let him in Sue, hi Tom come on in I want you to meet my dad, dad this is Tom my friend, hi Tom I heard you want to talk to me? Mr. Odell, I want you to know I love Sue and if she is pregnant, I well marry her, if it is ok with you and her mom, I care about her and the baby if there is one.

Tom would you like to have something to drink? that would be nice, we have tea and drinks I will take a coke ok, yes Sue get Tom a coke, ok mom now lets talk about this mess you and Sue have made of your lives, said her dad, what are you going to do about it? I know right from wrong, lets pray about this thing, I know God well take care of this, here Tom here is your coke. thank you, Sue, we well leave this in God. s hands, I have faith in him, young man do you believe in God? yes sir I do, that is good to know.

Sometimes we make bad judgement, we need God to clean this mess up, so we can go on with our lives. you and Sue I know can. t be the only one to make bad mistake, but God can do anything, we just need to do what God asked of us. I well pray for you both, tomorrow I will have my wife to take Sue to the doctor, it is getting late and we all need our rest, I will say goodnight, it is nice to meet you Tom, you to sir, thanks for the advice, see you all later bye Sue thanks for the coke Mrs. Odell Tom kiss Sue on her face and hug her, and left.

Mom do you know what change dad mind? He was real nice to Tom, I know honey, God can change many things, your dad wants the best for you, now lets go to bed, mom I heard dad asked Tom if he knew Jesus yes I heard that too, we well talk later tomorrow, now you make way to your bed don. t forget to pray, I have got to get up early to call your doctor, so you get to bed now goodnight mom goodnight Sue, when Sue got in her room, she felt like a little girl, down on her knees she fall the tears she could not hold back, dear lord I really need your help, if it is for me to be a mother at my age then you help me to be a good mother, with me so young and all, oh yes bless my friend Cindy she has been my good friend thank you lord for that. well lord I wont to thank you for good parents, amen, the next morning Sue heard her mom get up Sue, it is eight am, go answer the door I think it is your friend Cindy, you are right mom come on in Cindy, how did it go? We will have to talk later I have got to go to the doctor.

Ok Sue I well see you later bye Sue see you later Mrs. Odell in comes Sue mom you to Cindy you have a good day at School, thank you both have a good day said Cindy, Sue called me later after school. I will, mom I well be ready in a little, ok honey let's see if you can get in today I will call your doctor, when Sue went to her room, she was thinking I have got two people that really love me, my dad and mom, and I love them to so much, let me see what I have got to wear, I think this dress the blue one well be fine, Sue her mom was calling her, yes mom honey we need to leave we have got to be there at nine thirty, it is nine now, so hurry we do not wont to be late, I am almost ready, I am leaving ok mom I am right behind you. mom what if I am pregnant? do you think you are,

    The only thing I can say is I might be, I have not had a period in two months, mom it could be something else, if I am not pregnant I well not do that anymore, I am so sorry honey, it is ok let me tell you a story, about myself, I feel as you are lucky my dad was real mean to me, he found out I was with this boy, we were taken a picture up town in a booth his sister and me were good friends, she was with us a few kids from school was with us, we were having fun,. the picture we took was good I forgot left it in my book my stepmother found it, she gave it to my dad, he got all over me.

    He also was waiting on me when I came in from school, that was when he had his belt, he reached and grab me by my hair, he pull me to him, I well never forget that day, one of my worse times of my life, he pull my dress to the side, he hit me with that belt, on my backside, he told me I was never to go with that boy again, what did you say mom? reply Sue, well honey I knew better than to talk back, your grandpa did not want me to date anyone, why mom I guess I was to young, but he was not like us he was a mean man, I could not see my friend every again, I was to come home after School did you mom? yes I did because my stepmother she would tell on me, and I knew dad would get the belt after me.

My dad was mean to me, mom did you get to see your friends anymore? Except to meet on the street I could not see them, I did tell him I could not see him anymore, he was upset but that was how my dad put it to me, mom what happen after that? I moved back to my home town with my mother, I did not wont to be around my dad, mom I am so sorry, it is ok honey, I want you to know how good you have it with your family, here we are at the doctor's office., you set down the nurse will call you, as they enter the nurse came

After her mom sign her in, she was called, Sue Odell could you come here? Mom they calling me, Sue I need to check your weight, and blood pressure, and you need to go to the bathroom give me a sample of your pea, we need to check it, you can go to the waiting room now the doctor will call you in a little, while her mom feels out the papers what happen? did they lose your record?

I do not know mom, will they must have because I would not be felling out this if they had not, lost it, The nurse calls Sue mom. how do you wont to pay the bill,? I have cash reply Sue mom, I will call Sue when the doctor is ready, mom what did she say? I had to feel; out more papers, and I pay her, we well wait until she calls you,. mom I am real scared, I know how that feels, when I though about the picture in my book, what did he do with your picture, he tore it up, he would not let me keep it, mom you had a mean dad, I know I did, he is gone now, I do not miss him at all, how did he die? Well honey he drink smoke his self to death, Sue here is a gown put it on you mom can help you undress ., I n walks the doctor, my name is doctor Brown how are you? ok but what happen to doctor green? he had something to do, I see here your name is Sue Odell yes doctor, this is your mother yes it is, I see you are fifteen you are so young, is she going to have a baby?

said Sue mom, I am sorry but yes in seven more months, say she is almost three months gone.

Sue here is the time I wont to see you back in my office., are you going to keep your baby? I hope so we do not know yet,' said Sue mom, we well let you know we well talk it over, I have got to talk to her dad, Sue do you have any thing you need to asked me said doctor brown? If I decided to keep my baby well it be you are doctor green who well see me, yes we both can see you., I know your family I know your grandma to, wow I did not know that. well I have been here in this town for ever and it is such a little place, if you decided to give it up I know a couple they are nice.

This couple I know can not have children, they would love your baby I am sure, he works at the bank she does help him but they have a good income, and they could support it, we will keep you in mind, but right now we do not know, thank you doctor brown I paid before she saw you ok you are taken care of, when they got our side mom do you think I should keep the Baby? honey I need to talk to your dad, and you need to talk to Tom, you are young and you do not know one thing about babies, mom I do not want to give my baby to just anyone.

Mom when I get home. I well call Tom, I promised him I would, you can call him bur your dad and me will be the one to decide what we are going to do about the baby, that will be fine mom, when Sue enter there house she call Tom hello can I speak to Tom, this is his friend? Tom yes mother someone wants to speak to you, mother I well be right there. hello Tom yes this is Sue, hold on, mother could I have this call in private? Sure, I well *be* in the kitchen if you *need me,* ok mother, did you *see* the doctor Sue? yes Tom I did, are you pregnant? Yes, Tom I am, Tom was so excited let's get married, no we cannot I do not think mom is going to let me keep it, why said Tom? don. t I have anything to say? After all I am the father, will mom wants *me* to finished School, mom said I was to young to know anything about babies, Sue I well be at your house tonight, ok Tom, love you Sue me to said sue, bye Tom, see you later, mom I am going to lay down for a while, take me a little nap, are you tired yes mother? I well *be* up at five, I can help you with supper, that is ok Sue you need your rest,

*Sue* was laying on her bed she remember a party *she* was at, one of her old friends his name is Bob, she did not remember to much but she had dream about that party, when she walk in with her friend Bob, then bits and parts began to unfold she remember someone gave her a drink, Bob came over where she set, put his arms around her, the dream was so real, she put her arms around Bob, she saw lots of her friends the music was so loud everyone was dancing, so her and Bob began to joined the crowd, she was getting light head from what she drink, Bob may I lay down? I do not *feel* to good. she keep on dreaming Bob carried her to the bed room, he lay her down, she looked up at him he began to kiss her while he removed he clothes, Sue woke up. wow that is what happen, this baby is Bob, not Tom, she thought it was only a dream, no it is not it is real I need to go over to Cindy and tell her, this Baby belongs to someone else, not Tom, he would never understand.

Mom I want to go over to Cindy, what is wrong honey? Are you ok? nothing is wrong mom, it is tell me what is wrong? mom I just wont to go to my friends house, ok go on I well be back soon, Tom is coming over later, if he does make it here before me, tell him I well *be* right back, mom I will be ok don. t worry about me, as she kissed her mom bye, she was wonder what do I tell Cindy, she is going to think I am crazy, Sue got to Cindy she knock at the door, Cindy will you answer the door? and see who it *is*, mom it is Sue, will tell her to come on in, hi Sue how are you? Cindy, I have something to tell you can *we* talk in private?

Sue walked with Cindy to her room, hi Mrs. White, how are you Sue? you did go to the doctor, did you not yes Mrs. white I did, will what happen? are you going to have a baby? what did doctor green tell you? Mrs. white I did not see my doctor I saw doctor brown really, yes, and I am going to have a baby, how is your mom? She is upset, mom Sue come to see me she has something to tell me, come on Sue here is my room close the door, mom we will be out in a little, will what do you want to tell me Sue? this baby may be someone else, what are you saying? You remember me telling you about my friend Bob, and the party I went to? will we sleep together, and I think this could be his baby, are you sure?

I do not know but this could be a different story, what do you mean? I get you this Bob is same color as you yes? that is what I am saying, I know you love Tom, but this would be a horse of a different color, what are you going to tell Tom? you do not know this guy Bob? that much, do you know anything about him? No, it was a one-night stand, I meet him though a friend, the same night it happen, Cindy Tom is coming to our house tonight, it will give you time to talk, said Cindy, Cindy I do not want to talk to him tonight, but you must, does your mom know about Bob? no I came right over here after I got up, can I spend the night? I do not know what to do, will you call my house and tell mom I am spending the night I do not feel good, tell her to tell Tom see him later not now, I need to have some time along.

That is ok Cindy, I will go home, now and tell mom, I do not feel good, I will see you tomorrow, you going to be ok Sue? I need time by myself, time to think, you had better hurry because Tom well make it to your house before you, are you going to see Tom tonight? I plain on calling him and telling him we need to change our plains, I do not fell good I think after I talk to mom and dad I well take a bath and go to bed, so bye Cindy, when Sue got home, mom I have something I need to tell you, Sue heard her dad in the bathroom, mom dad is home? yes honey will good I will tell you both, tell us what honey? said her dad? Hi dad how was your day? ok what do you wont to tell your mom and me?

Mom before I talk to you and dad I need to call Tom, I need to call him right now, ok honey you do not need our permission to used the phone, Sue calls Tom, hello Tom I am so glad I caught you, before you left, yes what is up? I have got to change our plains, I do not feel to good, so I cannot see you tonight, could you make it tomorrow? ·sure honey that is ok I did have a test tomorrow, and I need to study, so it will work out for me, Tom I have got to go, see you tomorrow, I want to talk to mom and dad, have a good night, Sue hung up the phone, mom and dad you both have been great to me, and I want you to know how much I love you, we feel the same said her dad, mom and I want you to understand how hard this is for me to come forward and let you know what I found out, come on little lady what is up? dad and mom the baby is not Toms, what" you are good parents by showing me love.

And you were not bad to me when you found out I was pregnant, that is love, I think the baby is a friend of a friend of mind, we went to a party together, his name is Bob, would you listen to her Betty? Is he also white? No mom he is my color, it was a mistake, I have not, seen the boy since that night? no dad I have not, are you going to tell him? I guess after I brake Toms heart, dad he loves me, I know Sue I feel it, but it will be up to you about Tom, you know Betty our little girl is growing up, you are right Bob, she is so pretty, look at that long black hair, and black eyes, she looks like both of us.

And you were not bad to me when you found out I was pregnant, that is love, I think the baby is a friend of a friend of mind, we went to a party together, his name is Bob, would you listen to her Betty? Is he also white? No mom he is my color, it was a mistake, I have not, seen the boy since that night? no dad I have not, are you going to tell him? I guess after I brake Toms heart, dad he loves me, I know Sue I feel it, but it will be up to you about Tom. You know Betty our little girl is growing up, you are right Bob, she is so pretty, look at that long black hair, and black eyes, she looks like both of us.

Mom dad I need to get my bath, and go to bed, I am tired, Sue are you going to school tomorrow? I guess so I well call Cindy go to her house, mom dad goodnight honey you do not worry about what happen, God will help us to see the right way, do not forgot to pray, I will see you all in the morning ok Sue, said her mom, Bob yes Betty I was thinking of us taken the baby, what do you think? Will it is a thought, so how do you feel? we could talk about it, she is due in seven months, yes that is right, will we have that long to make up our mind, no we don't we need to know what we are going to do soon, we cannot wait the last minute, we need to talk to Sue I would like to take care of my grand baby, said Mrs. Odell.

Yes me to said her husband, Sue said she does not want just anyone to have her baby, she told me so said her mom, she is not to big so she want be showing to much, when she gets for a long, that is good said her dad, will it is bed time, and I am real tired, said her husband, we can talk about this later, with Sue, Tom is coming over and they will talk about the baby,., he will know it belongs to Bob, will I am tired we were at that doctor office for a while, I am so glad we know the truth.

The next morning Sue got up; she look at herself in the looking glass, she was looking at her stomach, one day it well be showing she said to herself, she heard her mom in the kitchen, mom is that you? Yes, it is breakfast is ready, mom I am getting ready for School, she did not hear her dad, mom has dad gone to work? Yes, he left early I do not think he got to much rest, mom I am going over to Cindy, not before you eat there is two of you now, I will not take no for an answer, ok mom Sue saw some toast on her plate she grab some before she left, bye mom see you after School, have a good day dear, you to mom, when Sue got to Cindy she knock at the door, mom someone is at the door, it is Sue dear come on in. how did it go last night? You did tell Tom about the baby, no we will be doing that tonight, change of planes, so I talk to mom and dad and went to bed.

Are you going to School Sue asked Cindy? Yes, I am, I need to leave now, sorry but I do not want to be late, have a good day, thank you Cindy you have a good day too, when Sue got to school, she could not get her mind off her baby, no one in her class knew she was going to have a baby, her teacher came to her desk, may I see you at the office Sue? Yes Mrs. Green, Sue began to look at her classmates they all had there eyes on her, she keep walking, when her and Mrs. Green got to the office, you can set over there said her teacher, I guess you are wonder why I asked you to come to the office? yes, I would like to know ok your mom and me talk, she told me you were going to have a baby and we both were worry about you, and the baby, with you playing ball. maybe you should not play, ok now are we finished? I would like to get back to my room, as they were walking back Mrs. Green was holding on to Sue hand, I was worry about you. that is ok seems as though mom was to.

When School let out Sue made her way home, I am home mom, how was your day dear? ok I guess I did find myself at the office, mom would you know anything about that.? Yes I do but I was worry about you and the baby, I only talk to Mrs. Green your teacher, the kids all look at me like they knew, I am sorry that is ok I understand where you are coming from, I would be the same way if it were me, but I was gone for a while, your dad well be here in a little while, we.have something we want to talk to you about, ok mom I will go to my room and lay down I am so tired, when dad gets home call me, yes dear I will, Sue goes and lays down, she had the same dream. this time it was different she remember Bob saying Doris when he lay her on the bed, what is that about my name is Sue, then she woke up that is just a dream she said to herself, he thinks my name is Doris why oh it is a dream.

When she got up, she heard her mom and dad talking, mom is dad home? yes dear he is, do you and dad still want to talk? Yes dear we will go to the living room, ha dad how was your day?, it was ok except you were on my mind, sorry dad Sue do not worry I pray for you, I know God will take care of you our physician is Jesus, he is with us always, I know dad, that is what I believe, we both love you *so* much and we want the best for the baby;, we want you to put your mind at ease we do not want you to worry, we know you do not want to give the baby to just anyone, with all being said we would like to take the baby, and raised l;t our self, mom that is cool, if it is ok with you, yes mom, you have my permission you can take care of my baby, are you sure? yes it may not be my baby but it could be my brother or sister.

So, you do not care said her mom? No like you said I do not know one thing about babies, and no one knows except the whites and doctor and my teacher, and Tom I forget him so it is settle mom the baby is yours and dads we can put that behind us, Sue it is time to eat come on Bob it is in the stove Tom, will be here soon, they all set down to eat, after they ate mom I am so tired, I am going to my room and lay down, for a while, honey are you all right, yes mom I just seems so tired all the time, you will be going back to the doctor in a few days, you need to tell him how you feel, mom it may be because there is two of us now that takes more, I will be ok, someone is at the door mom I am going to lay down, Sue it is Tom, I will get it come on in Tom she just lay down.

    Tom can I get you anything? I made a pie apple if you would like some, no that is ok, Sue had just lay down when you came up, I will get her, Sue Tom is here, I am coming mom, hi Tom how was your day? it was ok I guess, your mom said you were laying down, yes I have been real tired, but I will be ok, Tom I want you to know you have been a real good friend, I could not asked for anyone to be any better, when you found out about the baby you stood by me, you met my mom and dad you were nice to them, did not mind about the color of our skin, will I want you to know this baby is not yours, how do you know I just do, I am sorry but this conversation is over, I need to go lay down, I am sorry I did not want to hurt you.

    Wait Sue what is wrong? have I hurt you someway? why did you talk to me like that? a tear fall from Toms eyes, Sue don. t you know how I feel about you? Do you want to brake up with me? I guess I am I do not know how I fed anymore, give me some time I will call you, Sue do not let what we have disappear in to thin air, I know you do not feel good, Sue what about what we share with each other, Tom I need to go lay down I hope I did not hurt you I did not say it to hurt you, you can expect a call in a couple of days now I must go lay down, Sue mom walked with Tom to the door., she will be ok do not worry about her, bye Sue bye Tom, Tom left when he got out side what did I do,? Mom do not let anyone bother me, tonight; ok? I need to rest ok dear I will tell anyone that calls they can talk to you tomorrow, tell dad goodnight.

What was that all about said her dad? I do not know, I sure hope Tom did not think we had anything to do with her in what she said, she was real mean to him, I know said her husband, are you ready for bed? no I have got dishes to clean first, do you need help? no I can do them, I am so worry about Sue, she has never talk like that before, I think she just want it over in, walks Sue honey I thought you were in bed, I was but I could not go to sleep, mom I am sorry you to dad, I will! call Tom and say I am sorry, he was surprise; mom he was crying, yes dear you did hurt him, I did not mean to, he was upset I saw it myself, said her mom.

Dear go back to bed you need your rest, your dad and me will. be going to bed soon, ok mom I will, when Mrs. Odell went to bed Bob are you asleep? No why, I was thinking about our daughter birthday in a few days she well turn sixteen, she will be finishing school, I want so much to make her birthday nice for her, I thought we could have her a parry, for her invite her some friends, like Cindy her best friend, and some of her class mates, that would be nice dear, she has been *so* down, I will call Cindy and her mom, we can put things together, the next day sue heard her mom in the kitchen, she hurry and got dress, she did not want to be late for school, when she brush her teeth she went to the kitchen, mom what are you doing? Are you going to eat? your breakfast is ready mom I well have a glass of milk, and maybe a little of them eggs you have in my plate, set down you have time, I see dad has left yes dear he left early.

Mom these eggs are real good, thank you dear, I am glad you like them, are you felling better dear? I did get some rest, I will be going by to see Cindy after school, ok mom? Yes, dear will you be there long? Will mom I have been so tired and we have not got to do anything to much, but I will go by to see her today, and I will be home before dark, good dear, oh yes I will call Tom tomorrow, I promised him I would call, yes you did dear, got to go mom see you later have a good day dear, she kiss her mom on the face before she left, when Sue got to school, the kids look at her, one of her friends come to her, hi Sue how are you? ok I was wonder when we could get together maybe take in a movie are something, yes one day, she was thinking why now she never want to before, Cindy has been the only friend she has had.

While Sue was at School, she had her mind on the day Cindy and her found that money, she put her part in the bank, but she said to herself, I will need new clothes after the baby is born, she was still size eight but she knew she would gain some weight, she had her mind on' something else, when the teacher asked for her to come up front, yes Mrs. Green I will be right there, yes Mrs. green.

Sue will you still be coming to School when you start showing? I do not know ok I will visit your mom maybe she knows, the bell rings will it is time to go home have a good week end? See you Mrs. Green, I will see you Monday, said her teacher Sue left, she want to hurry get to Cindy it was on her way home,. she prayed dear lord help me to make the right decision in everything I do, help me to say the right words to Tom, amen.
When Sue got to Cindy she knock at the door, Cindy mom open the door hi Sue how are you? It has been some time since I saw you, I am ok how are you fine is Cindy home? yes she is I well go get her, in walks Cindy hi Sue how are you I am ok I came here from School, could we go for a walk?, let me tell mom., mom we are going for a walk ok don. t be long, I want mom, I do need help when you get back, ok mom, the two girls left, how have you been doing Sue? ok I did get some rest, that is good all at once Cindy fall oh no are you ok Cindy? as she got up off the ground yes I am ok, wow what happen? I do not know, I got a little dizzy, we better go back to your house, I am fine no you are not yes I am doctor, you do not look fine, have it your way Sue.

You take it easy until you see your doctor, Sue it is not that bad, why don't you wait for the doctor result? when they got to Cindy she open the door., Sue reach out for her. what you almost fall again, Sue call out to Cindy mom please come here, she was setting at the table what is wrong Sue? Cindy fall a while ago she was dizzy is that right Cindy mom I am ok., never mind I will make you appointment Monday, to see your doctor, you listen to your mom said Sue, yes doctor, will I have got to go I promised mom I would be home before dark, do you want to do anything tomorrow Cindy? since it is Saturday, I will called you I do not know how I well feel, ok bye, bye Sue, when Sue got home mom something is wrong with Cindy, what makes you think that? she fall we went for a walk and that is when it happen, and we went to her house and she almost fall again.

Mom I am going to call Tom, ok dear. You promised him you would, Sue calls hello Tom is this you? yes Sue it is how are you? I am ok how are you, ok before I say anything I want to apologize for the way I talk to you the other night, my mom and dad. said I was mean to you, I was just tired, but I cannot believe I talk that way, I hope you forgive me and we can still be friends, sure Sue I would like to stay friends, I was thinking about joined the service after I graduate is that what what you want Tom? yes I think so, good whatever you want but I have got to go take care of yourself, and let me know when the baby is born, I will never forget you Tom, I well never forget you Sue, we well talk later bye Tom bye Sue, dear what did Tom say? not much we will still be friends that is nice, dear.

Mom he well graduate soon he wants to joined the service, maybe he will like it dear, yes mom he wants to know when the baby is born, he should, mom here comes dad will I thought it was about time it is getting late, mom I am going to lay Down for awhile and rest yes dear you do that I well call you when supper is ready, hi how was your day Bob? ok it rain a little but I was ok Betty what did you do? Washed clothes and put some can goods up, good we can have garden food when we need it, *Sue* is laying down, she needs to rest, good you are right, she did talk to Tom he is still wants to be friends with her, good I, hope he would, also he wants to joined the service after School. that young man has got a good head on him I think you are right Bob.

Betty I need to 1 take my shower before we eat, Bob I put some towels and wash cloths in there for you, if you need anything else let me know, Betty what is for supper? I am cooking some chicken and mash potatoes and gravy green beans and to top it off Sue dish apple pie and ice cream good, now you hurry and get clean up before supper, maybe Sue will have her nap over, dear lord help me to do what you have me to do, for my family, I thank you dear lord, in walks her husband, will I feel better I feel clean, good said his wife, that chicken small good, it want be long until it will be ready, did you make my biscuits? Yes I sure did, Sue went by Cindy she said they went for a walk and Cindy fall, really what happen? they do not know, her mom is taken her to the doctor Monday.

I hope it is nothing serious said her husband, me to said his wife, honey would you move that plate so I can put the chicken in its place, sure I will do that, and would you check and see if Sue is still asleep? When Sue dad went to her room she was still in bed, she turn her head to the side, dad are you ok? Yes I was checking to see if you were up supper is ready, dad I will be there in a little, you need to hurry your mom has supper on the table, she will be here in a little, she just woke up ok I well put her plate next to yours, in comes Sue, mom that chicken sure smell good, Bob would you say the blessing? Dear lord I want to thank you for this food and thank for my family, everyone said amen, Bob do you work Saturday? No Betty I am off the whole week end, that is good you want to sleep in you can.

Sue do you feel ok? I know you have been tired, yes dad I feel better, dear tomorrow is Saturday what are you going to do? I do not know, your mom told me about your friend falling, yes dad while we were walking she fall, so sorry, your mom said her mom was taken her to the doctor, I am calling to see how she is, that is good you need to do that said her mom, Sue finished her supper and called Cindy, hello Cindy yes how are you doing? I feel ok, how are you Sue? I did get some rest. I went to sleep for awhile, before supper, are we doing anything tomorrow? I do not know it is still early I will? they are ok said Sue what about yours? They are fine, good willl I have got to go Cindy bye bye Sue., how is Cindy doing said her mom ok now.

Maybe she will be better after she see her doctor, mom did my teacher call you? no was she going to? She will call you Monday I think, what does she want dear? She will tell you, mom do you need any help with the dishes? No I can do them, you need your rest, in a few days it will be back to the doctor. so make sure you get all the rest you need, have you been taken your vitamins? yes mom every day, that is good dear, it is good for the baby, mom I will go to my room now, I will read some of my baby books, ok dear mom where is dad? He is in the living room watching TY, yes dear I will be going to my room to read, soon her husband joined her, Betty what do you want to do tomorrow? we could go shopping, if you want to dear.

Betty I am coming to bed, I am so tired, does the light bother you dear? I thought I would read a little, no I am going to sleep, he kiss his wife goodnight, the next morning Sue had got up, she went to the kitchen, her mom had breakfast cook, I have you some eggs dear in your plate and your bread is ready to be toasted ok mom thank you what are you doing today? I guess I will stay here till Cindy calls me, if she feels like going anywhere, mom are we going to church tomorrow? sure dear pastor Williams would wonder where we are at, yes and all the women in the singing would to, you are right dear, they would miss us, yes mom and I am sure they would miss dad, the brothers in church.

Mom my room needs cleaning, since it is Saturday I think I well see what I can do, I have got to go to School Monday though Friday so I do not have much time to clean, take it easy dear, I will mom, all I have got to do is my bed and clean the floor, everything else is ok, I need to make your dad. s breakfast, mom I will go get him. dad mom said your breakfast is ready, are you ready to eat? Yes I am coming, I am watching TV they have a tornado for our county, wait Betty look at the sky, it is all colors it is red green purple let me see dad?, dad that looks bad, yes it does, here it comes run for cover in the basement the wind pick up the kitchen door it came off the wind pick up thing they began to move in the yard, Mr. Odell saw it all before he ran for cover, they all began to pray, the house shook and the windows broke, my God said Sue we are all going to die, no we want said her dad God well take care of us.

Dad I wonder how Cindy is? I hope her and her family are ok, dear lord help us and all our family, and friends, take care of us, it seem like forever before the Odell could come out, they could not move the door, to the basement, help help said Mr. Odell, dad why can. t we move the door? it is stuck, is it Bob? Yes, Betty it is, someone well find us, I think the roof is still on, we still have our house, not to much damage, I think God took care of us, Bob I hear someone, is anyone in here? yes here we are said Sue, someone open the door, are you folks ok? Yes, we are said Mr Odell, well said the man who open the door it looks like everything is ok you did loose a back door, and some windows were broken, Mr. Odell look up saw a man with long hair and he need a shave he told his wife later, he told the ones that were with him to help him get these people out of the basement, they are all ok, and everything else is ok.

Are you sure everything is ok? Yes, said Sue, yes we are all fine thank God he, took care of us, you folks are lucky the ones next door lost the house and we cannot find anyone, so sad Dad. yes Sue you are right, there is lots of homes gone and we are looking for people that we cannot find, Dad lets go to my friend Cindy,?, ok dear go get in the car., no said the man, you people cannot go anywhere there or live lines ever where, you have got to stay put, we do not wont anyone to step on live wire and get hurt, maybe we can get things taken care of real soon, and you people can get back to your lives, thank you Mr in everything you all have done, Dad do you think Cindy and her family are ok? I am sure they are. but if you want try the phone see if it works, I will so Sue try no dial tone dad, I am sure they are ok, we will pray for them yes dad, we are ok just the kitchen door is gone.

Thank God it did not hurt us, bur dad I am worry about Cindy, I hope they are ok, me to said Sue mom, we all need co go to bed, it is getting late, mom the lights are off, we need to get the lamps out, Bob here is a candle light it and go get the two lamps out of the closet, this candle well be enough light to see the closet where the lamps are, Betty I will get them, give one to Sue and we need one for our room, Sue you blow it out before you go to sleep, ok dad, after you light it go look in your room to make sure everything is ok, ok dad it is see you both in the morning, I am going to bed, ok dear, the next morning the lights were still off, will I guess we well stay home, because we cannot go anywhere,. until we get the lights back on, then maybe the lanes well be off the ground.

I guess we will have to wait until the lights or on before we can cook, Bob if you and Sue are hungry, we have left overs some chicken and and other things left over from last night, no mom I will wait, me to reply her Dad, it still looks like it may rain, it does not matter the power company will still work, will I can clean my room, there is a little light, I can not read with no light, so I will clean my room,., dear someone is at the door, Bob see who that is, hello we are from the power company, we need to check your home to see if there i, any loose wire come on in, do you know how long it will be before we have lights,? We will get them on as soon a, we can, we just need to check before we turn them on, thank you sir, you are welcome, I do not see any damage that we have got to fix we should have them on in one hour.

My friend Cindy lives on Howard street you know on the corner in a brown house, do you know where that is? are you talking about the one where a red barn sets next to it?, yes that is the one, is it ok? No it is not it has some damage, windows are out roof some of it is gone, *so* no one is there I am sorry the people are missing, oh no replied Sue, she began to cry, I am sorry miss, that does not mean they are gone, they could have been taken to the hospital, we have got to stay put, how can I find my friend, honey we need to get our lights back on, once we get the lights back on I will go look at the house and see what is going on, and I will let you know thank you sir, she can not be missing,. I need to find her this is my job, I need to do this first., I promised to go check and let you know. maybe someone well know something.

The power man left, I will be back when I find out something, honey do not worry about Cindy, said her mom, I am sure she is ok, the man said he would be back, maybe he will flnd Cindy, I know God will take care of her, mom I am going to my room, and pray for my friend, God control the weather, put her in God hands, I am sure she well be ok said her mom, when Sue got to her room she got down on her knees and prayed, dear lord please take care of my friend Cindy, and her family thank you lord amen, when she got up the lights were on. she ran to the kitchen to tell her mom, good I am glad now I can fix you two something to eat, mom I am ok no you are nor, you stop crying you have the baby to think about.

Sue you sat down I have you and your dad some eggs fix, you both have not eat, we can not do anything except wait on the lord, ok mom that will work, mom have you are dad seen bingo?, not since before the storm he is not here dear,? no mom I will look out side and see if he is here, ok dear, mom he really liked Cindy you don't think he went there do you? mom I do not know, he could have he ha, went with me many times to her house, he may thought I was there, will you both need to eat come on dad mom has us something to eat coming, Betty you need to eat to, I have me a plate made, ok set down and eat, I well.

Someone knock at the door, mom I will get it, mom it is the power man he is back, miss I went to your friend house, no one was there, it is a mass, no one can live there, until it is worked on, the windows are out part of the roof is gone, I found something, does your friend have a dog? no why because I found one at her house, what color is it black and white that is my dog bingo, here he is come here bingo, why would you go away from us,? Mr thank you I have got to feed my dog, and give him some water, it has been awhile.

Mom do you know where bingo food is? look under the table, I know he is hungry mom and he needs water, I wonder why he went to Cindy? I do not know, mom, *he* did like Cindy, she has her way with dogs, morn I am going to try the phone see if it works, I well get the phone book and see if I can find the hospital number, here it is mom, the number, is it working dear the phone is but no one is answer the ring, hung up try back later, ok mom I will, mom the news is on this is Tom green out of Georgia there has been a tornado hit Howard county lots of homes have been destroyed many people are missing, Roy green is standing on Howard street Roy what is going on Tom I am standing next to a home that is flat on the dirt, they can not find the home owners, Mrs could you tell our views what happen? well my name is pat Johnson. my husband and me were in our home. when we saw it coming toward us. we ran for cover. just before it hit. thank God we are ok, yes Tom it is a mess back to you, will that is the news, out of Howard county, people watch when you are on the highway, we have look for people we have not found.

Mom I wonder if the number for the hospital is still not working? I do not know try it, ok I will., mom there is still no answer,., will dear they probably having to look at lots of sick people from the storm, mom I wish I could find out what is going on, I hate staying at home not knowing anything, I wish I knew someone to call that might know what happen to Cindy, and her family, Mom do you remember when Cindy and me were little? yes dear what about it, will it has been some time we both are a lot older, yes dear, will we do not spend time together, and her mom and you do not spend time together, like you all did when we were real little, you are right dear we will have to go out to eat are shopping yes mom I know her mom would like that, you two were real close, yes we were, mom I am going to watch TV, the news is on, we have got some new information on the storms that hit here Saturday this news is out of Georgia, my name is Tom green, there was a tornado hit our little town, in Howard county we have some of the people here that lost there family.

We have a lady here what is your name? my name is Brenda Johnson we are talking to Brenda, Johnson she lost her family in that bad storm, she is so upset, with tears in her eyes, miss I am so sorry but could you tell our views what happen? We live on lake street, my husband and me, God did take care of us, I call my mom, and no answer, we are standing here in front of her parents house, miss what then when we could not get them on the phone we rush over here and my mom and dad were under a pall of junk, I have told my mom to come to our house when something happen like this, we have a basement that is where my husband and me were, thank you miss, she is taken this real hard loosing her family, so many more they have not found, Tom we give it back to you thank you Rick mom that is so bad, I know dear mom that is the same street Cindy lives on, I know dear, what if she did not make it?_ I am sure God took care of them.

Mom is dad laying down? yes but I need to get him up I have got to washed some clothes and I need to washed what he has on, it is almost night time he will go back to bed Bob get up I need to washed the clothes you have on, ok I will give them to you, I am going back to bad, I have got to work tomorrow, ok dear do you want anything to eat? no dear I will be ok, I am getting my clothes washed and I will hung them on they line tomorrow, mom I can do that for you if you like? There well not be any School tomorrow, I am sorry dear I know how you like School, that is ok mom I can help you while I am out.

Mom I am going to bed, I well see you in the morning, ok dear, you have a good night, we have a big day tomorrow, yes mom I want to find Bob, dear do you want to tell him? I thought since your dad and me are taken the baby, you would not tell him, but mom I want him to know, good night mom we will talk later, it is dose for now, do not forget to pray, ok mom, when Sue got to her room, she got down on her knees, she prayed, dear lord please find Cindy, she is my best friend, keep her in your arms,. and her family amen, well I guess I will get my rest now. it is dark out side, we have been though so much thank you lord for good parents.

The next morning, Sue got up, got dress, she hear her mom in *the* kitchen, mom I was thinking since I am not going to School and I hope you do not have things to do maybe you could carried me to look for Bob?, we can do that but you need to eat yes mom I see you have my eggs already in my plate, yes and you need to drink the milk I pored you that is for the baby, it well keep the baby healthy, so you drink all of it, then we will hung the clothes on the line, God gave us a pretty day, Sue, what time do you want to go find Bob? As soon as we do what we need to do, ok dear you go get my keys, on my dresser, then we will from the yard, when we finished, doing the clothes, we will go. mom the place we will go to is the same place he had the party at. it is on dream street about one mile from here, lets go we are finished, dear what is Bob last name? it is Jones mom.

Does Bob work? mom I do not know, what we had was a one night stand, I saw him that night and we have not seen each other again, and if someone had not put something in my coke I would not see him now, mom I see dad left early, yes dear he had something to do, you know he works at the sock factory?, yes mom I do dad don. t keep secret from me, he has been there around thirty years, that is a long time, mom why did you not used the dryer that dad bought you last Christmas?, we could have but I like for them to get God. s sunshine, they smell good, but mom on the clothes line everything gets on them, and it is hot should be a good day for them to dray, said her mom.

Turn here mom on marshal street, it will bring you to dream street, he lives here in the house on the corner, pull in this drive way, I will see if he is home, ok dear, Sue knock at the door, a man with black hair open the door. he look like he was ready for some sun, with his shorts on, hi my name is Sue Odell, do you remember me? I am sorry, what did you say your name is? You may not remember me but you asked me for a date, after my friend got us together, then you asked me to come to your party, now you remember? Yes I do, how are you? I am ok why the visit? I have something to tell you.

Remember we were together that night? Yes, you are going to be a father, what I am pregnant how do you know it is mine? Because I do know, will when is the little tad going to be born? I went to the doctor he said the baby would be born in seven months, that was one month ago, so it will be in six months, yes that is right, let me know so I can come and see it, are you going to keep it,? no my mom and dad are going to raise our child, oh no that is not going to happen, I well take you to court, you,. can not take care of a new born, I will get me a lawyer I will to ok we will see each other in court, fine you had better let me know when it is born, Bob you well loose, you can not take care of a baby.

There is nothing else to say, I well leave, you had better let me know when that baby comes, I am fighting for it, I am getting married, then I will have someone to take care of it, we will see she had a tear in her eye, she was so upset, when she got to the car, what is wrong dear? why are you crying? He wants my baby, I tried to stop you from telling him I knew what was going to happen, he does not want to pay child support, but mom I told him you and dad were raising the baby, he did say he was getting married, so someone could help raise the baby, do not worry we well pray about this, he was so mean when he found out about the baby, do not let this upset you, I promised I well talk it over with your dad, mom watch there is still things on the road.

Mom could we go by the hospital, I want to see if Cindy is there, I need to find out so I can know if she is ok, mom pull over there, I well go to the front desk, so that is what Sue did, miss can I help you? yes I hope you can, I am looking for my best friend, she may have been caught in that terrible tornado, that came Saturday,

I well check, what is your friend name Cindy Sue white, yes I see we do have her here, is she ok, do you know why she is here? Will she was in that storm and we have been running test on her, she is on floor 326 the third floor I do not think she can have anyone except her kin, but you can asked her nurse, her name is Judy green miss I need to go tell my mom; so she well not be worry, ok miss.

Mom she is here, I want you not worry, because I might be here for awhile, do you want to go and see her? no I will stay here you try and hurry, Sue, goes back in, she was thinking I go this way to the third floor, and turn left, I see it now. miss can I help you I am looking for Judy green that is you I see your name tag, yes that is me what can I help you with? do you have anyone that was admitted to this hospital, Saturday name Cindy Sue White, let me check, yes we do are you her kin no but we are close friends, I want to make sure she is ok, come with me, how is she we are running some test on her, she is not to good, may I see her, sure come on she is in that bed in front of you, Cindy are you ok? Cindy moves her head to the right are you ok, yes how did you find me? was worry and I look here first. and asked question, the power man told me your house look real bad.

I am ok you are not, I talk to your nurse, she said they were doing test on you, Sue do you know where my parents are? no don.t you? how would I know when I did not know you where here, I just found you, do you think they are here? I can asked if you want me to, yes would you? I am worry about them, they should have told you before now, said Sue, before I asked I want to asked you something, guess who was at your house after the storm, I do not know, was someone there? how could it be? no one could live there, from what you said, not a human no you are right, than what,? It was Bingo, your dog yes what was he doing there? I do not know, the power man found him, after I asked if he would see how you were, and your family see if you all were ok, he thought it was your dog, you know Bingo does like you, now will you go check on my parents if they are here. I will be right back, ok thanks, yes miss do you need more help, it was that same nurse that show her where Cindy was, could you tell me is Cindy mom and dad are here? what is there names Ruth and her husband is Joe white.

I well let you know in one minute Sue had a seat come here miss I found your friend parents, are they ok? yes they do have some broken bones, and some bruises, not to much more I do nor think they are as bad as there daughter, she may have surgery oh no why? I can not tell you only her family, oh the parents are on the forth floor her mom is room 401 and her dad 402 I well tell her that, she well be glade to know where they are, could you tell them about Cindy that she is in the same hospital they are at, yes I can I well call her nurse, Sue goes back to Cindy room, did you find them? yes they are here, the nurse is going to let them know you are here, thank you Sue, you are welcome, now I have got to go, mom is waiting for me in the car I well see you tomorrow, ok did you get with the baby dad? yes that is another story I have got to go Sue lean over Cindy and hug her see you later love you take care love you to Sue, now I can sleep better knowing you are close by.

Cindy try to get some rest, Sue left I am so glad she is ok, when Sue got to the car, I am sorry mom but I had to talk to Cindy, is she ok dear well mom she may have surgery what is wrong? mom they well not tell me, they have been doing test on her, I need to call her later before dark, and mom well you take me back to see her tomorrow? ok but lets go home I am tired, do you need anything from the store Sue? No mom we can go home, I need to feed bingo and give him some water, and I well take in the clothes off the line they should be dray, back at home your dad is home I see his truck in the yard, let me get the door for you mom, Sue open the door, mom are you telling dad what Bob said, yes why not he needs to know.

How was your day Bob? ok I did work a little over time, I well get supper done, where have you and Sue been, we found Cindy at the hospital, and Sue visit with her a little, how is she? they are doing test on her, did she not get caught in the storm? yes she did, she was already sick though, mom I am going and get the clothes and bingo come and go with me I well feed and water you when I get the clothes off the line, bingo come on now you well tear the clothes I know you are glade to see me, mom I need to feed and water bingo ok dear but you lay down after don't you need some help in the kitchen no I can do it but mom  never mind said her dad you listen to your mom you need rest ok dad, I well get you up when I get supper done, the baby need you even now rest, you do not wont me to put the clothes away, no I well do it later.

Bob remind me to tell you something later?, ok I am going to see if sue went to sleep I know she is tired after the things we did today, she wants me to take her back to see Cindy tomorrow, don't you think it well be good for her to be around her friend? Said her dad, and don't she have school tomorrow, I can take her when she gets out around three I plain on picking her up at school, she is worry about Cindy, you know dear they have been friends for so long. it has been fifteen years so for they were raised together, like sisters, said his wife, yes I guess you are right Betty, dear go get her, tell her supper is done, Sue your mom has supper done thanks dad I well be right there, as Sue enter the kitchen mom that sure smell good that is what your dad said.

Mom would you pass the butter? I want some on my potatoes sure dear, you have two to eat for now, you go ahead and stuff your self, you are so little, no one will notice, if you gain weight, and it will help the baby, yes mom it will be a healthy baby, speaking of baby, Bob we went to see the babies dad today, you what?, why Sue, dad I wanted him to know, what he had done to me, someone put something in my coke, I see dear what did he say to you, After you told him,? dad he wants the baby, he can not have it, I know dad, he said he would get married to get the baby, so he could have someone to help him raised it, he would go that for?, I guess so, he said he would see us in court, I have heard enough we will leave it in God. s hands, dear would you say the blessing? yes dear I will.

Dear lord thank you for the food you have given us, and the love that has keep us together, be with my family the rest of the week, and let us never forget where we came from, and the blood you shed for us amen, now lets eat, and enjoy each other company, we well give it all to God that is to big for us, mom dad I well go to bed now see you both in the morning, ok dear you sleep good said her mom, I love you both we love you to dear said her dad, and do not forget to pray, when Sue got to her room. she got down on her knees to pray, dear lord thank you for finding my friend Cindy, lord I pray she well be ok, thank you lord for my parents, that have stood by me, thought I have done things that is wrong, I need forgiveness from you amen.

When Sue got up off her knees, she said to her self! forgot to call the hospital, and check on Cindy, mom yes dear I forgot to check on Cindy, I thought you call the hospital already, no but I well now Sue rang the number, hello you have reach south east hospital, my name is Jeanie brown yes I am trying to find out how my friend Cindy white is, what is your name my name is Sue Odell yes I remember you today you were here yes that is right, well honey your friend is not to good, she is in line for a kidney what is she ok? well she is asleep right now we are looking for a donor, I well see her tomorrow after school, ok dear have a good night, you to said Sue, what is going on said her mom? something wrong with Cindy? mom she needs a kidney, she can have one of mine, are you sure dear yes mom, she is my best friend she would do for me.

Mom I am worry about Cindy, she will be ok dear, we will pray for her, mom I am going to bed now, I have got to go to school, and after school I want to go see Cindy, ok dear I well rake you, I wonder if her parents know, mom it is worse than I thought, good night mom good night Sue, have a good night, you to mom, Sue went to bed, dear lord please let my kidney be ok for Cindy?, she needs help, I put her in your hands, thank you lord, Sue went to sleep the next morning she heard her mom in the kitchen, many times she has heard her fixing breakfast, good morning mom, good morning dear did you sleep ok,? J had Cindy on my mind till I went to sleep. I miss her mom, she will be ok dear, mom I well eat my eggs and then I have got to go to School, mom I see dad is gone yes dear he is, he left early.

Sue went to her room to get dress, she still had her friend on her mind, while she was getting ready she saw the dress she wanted to wear the blue one, her and Cindy had one of the same, she remember when they wear them on the same day. Cindy gave her a pin to wear it was still there where she had put it, wow time sure fly by fast, well I have got to put my thoughts aside and go to School, mom I well be waiting on you bingo mom well feed you you can not go with me this time, see you tonight, Sue reach down and pet bingo

Bingo here is some food, you can not go with Sue she is going to School, I know you are hungry you are a good boy, on Sue way to catch the bus she walked by Cindy house, what a mess the house look so bad, Sue said to her self it was the hand of God to keep them safe well I have got to get to School, here comes my bus, when Sue got on the bus, she was looking at the children, and they were looking at her, when she got to school she went to her room, and set down, she heard the bell ring. for school to start, ok you children take out your spelling book we have a test this coming up this week, hope you have been studying for it Sue did not have her mind on the spelling test, after what she knew about her friend she was crying, *the* teacher knew something was wrong, Sue would you come here? Sue went to find out what her teacher wanted, is anything wrong Sue?

Yes miss green, you know that my friend Cindy and her family were in a bad storm and her and her family are at the hospital, she was sick before she went to the hospital, she has got to have a donor for a kidney transplant, that has got me upset, I wont to give her one of mind, you do yes miss green, Sue had tears in her eyes, I miss her so much, I am sure you do, you can go back to your seat, Sue would you like for me to call your mom? Would you miss green? My mom is coming after school today to pick me up she was going to take me to the hospital, ok she can come early I well call her, I well let her know to come pick you up now, Sue went to set down the kids look at her so sad, even though Sue was felling bad, it made her feel good to know the kids were felling sorry for her, she got the tears off her face, and set down, Sue your mom is here you may leave see you tomorrow, get your things.

It seem so long for her mom to pick her up, now remember you well have a short day it is Wednesday tomorrow yes miss green see you then, you belive in God he well take care of you, and your friend, Sue saw her mom in the car, I have got to go, Sue left, when she got to the car mom I am so upset, about Cindy, that is why I am going home early, I am sorry dear, you do not have to worry we well be at the hospital in a little. you do not wont Cindy see you crying, yes mom you are right, Sue is it all right if I drop you off and come back in thirty minutes,? Yes mom that is ok, I wil be back soon, you have some time with your friend, give her a big hug for me, ok mom I well.

Sue got to the hospital went to the third floor, she talk to the nurse, how are you miss, I am ok, I do feel sorry for my friend, she was awake early she will be glad to see you, she said you were coming to see her today, yes I told her I would, is she ok,? no honey she is not, does she know what is wrong with her? no but we are going to tell her, that is what we were talking about early, how we would do it, we are going to tell her parents first, we are going to tell her family now, do you want to go with us? I would loved to, ok come on we are going now, so Sue went with them to tell Cindy family, it was on the forth floor room 401 and 402 the nurse went to 402 get Mr white bring him to his wife room we want to get you together the doctor has something to tell you about your daughter Cindy, doctor stone these are Cindy parents Mr and Mrs white the doctor must speak to you now, we have got to find a donor for your daughter she needs transplant for her kidney your daughter is real sick, we must act now, Mrs white she can have.

Sue are you sure dear? *Yes* Mrs white I am, we are friends I would do anything for her, I know she would do the same for me, we all are going to Cindy room and tell her, doctor stone is going to tell her, said the nurse, he wants you all to be there she is going to need you all, lets go the nurse went first, miss are you asleep? no I am awake, your parents want to see you, and you doctor stone has got something to tell you, your best friend is here, Sue goes over to Cindy, hugs her neck I have to hugs one from me one from my mom, you give your mom a big hug for me ok I will how are you doing,? I guess they did lots of test on me since I have been here Cindy your doctor needs your time now, miss I have bad news for you what? we did some test on you and we found out you need a transplant for a donor on your kidney mom come here ok dear everything will be ok, your family are here for you said doctor stone Honey you well be ok they both had tears in there eyes, God well take care of you,. that is one of his promised, Cindy I will give you one of mine, you would do that for me? yes I would, we are friend you would do it for me, I am going to give you one of my kidney if we match, they will take a little blood from me, and if it match we well have you a kidney, now I have got to go my mom is waiting on me, it has been thirty minutes, since she has been gone, I pray we will be a match. I owed you my life said Cindy, you are my best friend for ever I want to do it, Cindy mom and dad went over to Sue put there arms around Sue if you every need anything you let us know, I will say bye for now see you tomorrow Cindy ok Sue.

Sue got to the waiting room she saw her mother, she could not hold back the tears, as she ran to meet her, what is this more water works? Mom I need for you to approve to give Cindy one of mine kidney, is that what you want you wont to do dear? yes mom she is my best friend in the whole wide world, ok but we need to go home and talk this over with your dad, mom I well do the test tomorrow, the blood test, mom we need to call my teacher and let her know that I well not be at School tomorrow, they wont me at the hospital early so they can do the blood test before I eat. that is what the doctor said, I really miss Cindy mom I know you do. little girl we are here I well go and call your teacher, ha bingo said Sue, what are you doing he began to wag his rail as if to say he was glade to *see* her. I well get you some fresh water, come on and drink Sue I got in touch with Mrs. green your teacher, she said not to worry she would see you when you got back to School.

Mom I am tired I need to go lay down ok dear, Sue I do need to talk to the doctor, about you being pregnant well I guess its ok. to call him we need to know, if it is all right to do the test, *so* her mom rings the hospital number, hello I am calling about one of your patient at the hospital, what is her name? Cindy she needs a kidney transplant, my daughter she wants to see if she is a match, I need to talk to doctor stone, what is your name? Betty Odell ok hold the line he well be with you in a little, I did catch him at the hospital, hello this is doctor stone how can I help you? my name is Betty Odell I am Sue mom she was there today visit one of your patient, that has got to have a kidney transplant I remember her, we had talk, yes what I need to know is if it is ok to do the test since Sue is pregnant, sure it is ok it well only be a blood test, not a x ray I told Sue I would asked you ok Mrs. Odell it is fine, your daughter is going have a baby? She is six months gone, I think.

Sue I did talk to doctor stone he said it is ok for the test, you are to be at the hospital at six am in the morning, that is early yes dear but if you are a match they well do the transplant after the test, I pray that I am mom, and Cindy well be ok, me to dear, do you want a sandwich? you have not eating anything today except at breakfast, ok mom you talk me into it, here is you a sandwich now eat it, I need to get in bed early so I can get my rest. and do not worry I well be with you all though the procedures said her mom thanks mom if I every need you it will be then, I thank your dad well want to be there to, how is your sandwich? it is good mom.

Mom I think dad pull up in the yard, I will go to the door and let him in, mom it is dad, hi dad how was your day? Ok what about you and your mom what did you both do, dad I went to School but I could not do my work so, my teacher called mom she came and pick me up, we went to the hospital, to see Cindy, how is she dear? Nor to good, dad she has got to have a donor for a kidney transplant, yes dear I am so sorry, Betty what did you do, like Sue said we were at the hospital, Bob I need to asked you something, what dear, Sue wants to give Cindy one of her kidney, Sue is this what you want? what about the baby,? mom called doctor Stone Cindy doctor, he said it was ok, we are to *be* at the hospital at six am in the morning, then we will know if Sue well match what.

That is easy, yes that is what the doctor said, Bob do you want to be there? I guess I can get off work, I well call and see, ok you do that Sue while I fix supper can you make sure everything is ok for tomorrow, make sure your clothes is on the bed for in the morning, mom I well lay down for awhile call me when supper is ready, ok dear I well, Bob has made his call to find out if he can be with his family at the hospital, dear it is ok for me to be with you all at the hospital, that is good dear, Bob you can watch TV while I finished supper. ok dear, I think I will read my bible, I need Gods help so much, his word well be the tool, I need it to start my day tomorrow, it well be a long day tomorrow, I need to go by the bank and get some cash for us, you are right dear, I am reading my bible now ok supper well be done soon, mom I hope everything goes all right for Cindy me to dear.

I thought you were laying down Sue? I was I could not rest I had my mind on Cindy, she is on my mind all the time, I can. t wait till she is better, she well have a kidney mine, yes dear we can get our lives back together, Bob yes Betty,? I was thinking about Cindy mom and dad, and Cindy, staying with *us*, they have no home since the storm destroyed there house, yes dear if that is what you want, they well be like family, because she will have our daughter kidney that is right dad we will be sisters, it would be like I help my sister out with a kidney, so it is ok Bob? sure we could let them stay with us, Cindy mom is your friend?, yes that is right, will we can try if you like, but Bob it well be awhile the two girls well spend sometime in the hospital, till they get will.

We are here mom lets go in, the hospital, mom I well be back that is where I check in, ok dear, can we help you said that same nurse that was waiting on Cindy and helping her to eat and also Sue remember her talking to her, I am Sue Odell we are here to do the test to find out if I can be a match for Cindy a donor she needs a kidney, yes you are right, you can come with me mom come on this is my mom hi said the nurse, doctor stone well talk to you before the test, you both can set down, he well not be long, thank you, mom what is going on I do not know I am sure he well explain, the door open hello doctor Stone this is my mom, hello well this is the day, are you ready Sue yes doctor, what do you need to tell me? Before we do the test we like to talk to the donor, if you match with Cindy, white we well start the operation, it well take a couple of hours, maybe more or less, you both well be close.

Is that it? yes we will start now you will be ok said the doctor, in comes the nurse from the lab, I guess you know who I am we well need a little blood for the test, give me a tight fist, it well sting a little ouch sorry we are finished, you both can go to the waiting room,. the nurse well call you in about one hour, could I go to Cindy room? Sure go on visit your friend, don. t leave the hospital, we wont?, mom dad is back. dear I well go where he is if you wont to come, to Cindy room the number is 326 I well wait on you, when Sue got to the room Cindy ate you asleep? come on in how are you? I am ok, I did the test, I guess we well know if our blood match, so you had the test? It well be one hour before we know.

My mom and dad are here, they will be here in a little, dad pull up before I came to your room, you are such a good friend said Cindy well we have been friends for a long time, there is nothing I would not do for you as well, that is what I told my mom, said Sue, you were saying something the other day when you were here about Bob, and the baby yes he wants my baby, he does? yes he said he would take me to court, what are you going to do Sue? Well I told mom and she told dad, we are ready for what every he starts, he is not getting my baby, I only told him so I could explain why it happen, what are you talking? AboutWhat happen? Someone put something in my coke, I was not drinking, I do not drink, it put me in a loving mood, and he knew I was drunk, so that is what happen, so you told him? Yes I did, someone is knocking at the door, come in said Cindy in walk Sue mom and dad, how are you Cindy? Ok Mrs. Odell since my best friend is here with me and her family are.

Well it is getting close to one hour since they did the test, they well be calling for us soon, yes I guess you are right, said Sue, in walks the nurse miss the doctor well see you now, the test are back you need to come with me, this room you can wait, the doctor well see you in a little, ok mom here is where we well wait where is dad? He is in the waiting room, he said we could let him know what the result is if the blood type match, he would wait, mom I am scared, you hold it everything is going to be ok God well work out things for us, you think you well be helping your best friend, if the blood match, yes mom you are right, I well be ok, in walks the doctor with his papers on the test, Sue your blood type match now we wont to get things ready to do the operation, are you ready? Yes doctor, in walks the nurse, ok Sue we well get things going, we well get the room ready, you stay here, I well go get Cindy ready so we can start.

Sue got close to her mom and dad, the nurse went to Cindy room, are you ready? The rest that Sue took pass she has the same type of blood you have, so we are getting things ready for the operation, now said Cindy, yes now, we will get you both ready for the kidney transplant now could you raise up so I can put this gown on you it opens in the back. that is what we want, ok nurse, now I am giving you a little shot to make you want to go to sleep, before we start the procedures, ok nurse someone is getting Sue ready you both will be in the operator room at the same time, they are ready, here comes Sue and here we go to the operation room hold on it is cold down here said Sue, yes said Cindy when they got where they were suppose to go the doctors were there, bring them pretty girls here, we will get started, all right girls time to say goodnight., you will be out for awhile, count back from a hundred you both, back at Sue mom dear lord be with our little girl and us amen.

Are you ready said doctor Stone? Yes doctor the nurses ok everyone lets get started, nurse hand me the scalpel is there blood pressure ok nurse green ok doctor, doctor brown how is your patient doing.? Ok doctor stone, I need something for blood nurse green how is the blood going? Everything is ok doctor stone will we can close them up, the transplant was successful, they well be out for awhile, I well go tell there family, nurse green would you please bring the familys to my office so I can talk to them,? Ok doctor, the family were in the waiting room they saw the nurse Mr and Mrs Odell would you come with me and also Mr and Mrs white come to nurse bring them, this is doctor Stone office would you all wait for the doctor here he is now, Mr and Mrs white and Mr and Mrs Odell the operation is finished it went real good the girls are ok they will be in the recovery room in thirty minutes, you well see them then, they stay in the hospital well be a few days, so they are ok ask Sue mom yes they are and now Cindy should recovery good she has a kidney from her best friend Sue, saved her.

Thank God they came though it ok. now all we do is wait, Betty do you think they well be long in the hospital? A few days I am sure, I well miss my little girl said Sue mom, me to said her dad, but she is happy to help out her friend, I know dear, now they can get there lives back together, they have know each other forever, will it is almost time to see them yes said Cindy mom I know she well fell better, I want to thank you all so much for what you have done for my little girl, Sue, you so brave yes we know but they are like sisters, that is what Sue said reply her mom, will if Sue every needs anything she can come to *us,* she will get it she saved our daughter life, we owed her so much, will I see the nurse she is coming to take us to the recovery room to see our daughters, Mr and Mrs white will all come with me the girls are asking for you all,? Ok here we come so they are ok yes they are this is where they are at mom dad here we are, both of there parents went running how are you said Cindy mom? we are ok mom will do you both feel ok yes we do I am a little sore said Sue me to they just gave us some pain medicine, so we are ok for awhile.

Sue yes mom your dad and me are going to the house, we will be back tomorrow, will you be ok yes mom, ok we will be here in the morning, around ten ok yes mom, if you need anything you tell the nurse she will take care of you, we are so glad you could help your friend with a kidney, me to said Cindy, I was on my way out that is what doctor Stone said, I do believe that God could heal you, don. t you know that, yes Mrs Odell I do but sometimes God wants us to try another, way with this it was my one and only best friend, that stood in for me now I will be ok yes you will said Sue, and you know Sue I would do the same for you, yes I do now I am going try and rest said Sue Cindy you need to rest to, said Sue ok mom they can take you and dad back to your room, the nurse is coming to get you and dad now see you both in the morning goodnight said Cindy you to dear as her mom and dad kiss her on the face you rest now dear you to Sue, I will.

I thought they would never leave said Sue, I know said Cindy, Sue you are the best friend ever, thank you Cindy I am so glad that our blood match, me to, I was so scared, I could not get this day off my mind said Sue, I prayed about it, me to reply Cindy, I guess I did not have enough faith, I want to trust God, but my mom had more trust than I did, she prayed to about the test and that we would be ok, Cindy I want you to know I like you as a grate friend we played together, Cindy do you remember the day you and I was waiting on mom and you were waiting on your mom you had to go to the bathroom, some white man told me to get off the bench, you came out of the bathroom at about the time it happen you asked me what he said, I was crying because I did not understand what was going on you went to your mom and and my mom to see why he had said that, you did not get any answer, yes I remember no one could tell us anything.

Yes also there was another thing that same day I got hit by a car remember Cindy?, yes I was with you to give you support, when it happen, I could hear you telling me to hold on and that I would be ok, you prayed for me yes I did and you came to see me with my mom, you bought me a doll I named, after you, yes you did, do you still have that doll? yes I do it is in my room along with the rest of my things, I well keep it forever, yes I also gave you a pin for your dress we both have the same dress, that is right said Sue, I was looking at mine the other day. it brought back the time we wear them together, we have lots in coma you and me, will lets go to sleep talk to you tomorrow ok goodnight Sue goodnight Cindy. The next morning Sue mom got up, Bob we have got to get ready if we want to be at the hospital by ten am, ok I am getting up I will go make brcakfa.st, ok that will give me time to read my bible, good said his wife, I guess I will make eggs and bacon it will be ready soon, I wonder how Sue is this morning? Well yesterday she seem ok after they got to recovery, yes they did said his wife, Bob breakfast is ready come and eat, I am coming, we can leave here at a little after nine and be there close to ten, are you ready Bob? Yes Betty I am we will not be there long, I told them we would visit them today, ok said Bob, how is your eggs and bacon? Ok I was hungry, me to I know I will miss my little girl, me to said her husband, I need to feed Bingo come on boy, here is your food and water, Bob I think he is missing Sue me to Betty.

I am though eating, we can go now, ok Bingo you be a good boy, he wag his tail to let her know he understand what she said Sue will be home soon, she missing you, I am sure, will lets go, I will stack the dishes and wash them, when I get home, at the hospital, I wonder where mom and dad are it is almost ten/ They will be here Sue, did you sleep ok? Yes what about you Cindy? I am ok I was thinking where well we live when we go home? Don't worry Cindy my mom and dad have that work out. they will be talking to your mom and dad about that, ok I will wait and see what happen, did you eat you food? Yes a little Said Sue, I called about a shot I was having pain, me to you were asleep when I woke up so I let you sleep, here comes your mom and dad with flowers pretty, mom you and dad did not have to bring them we want to and here is some for you Cindy, thank you very much, you are welcome, this will put a pretty spot in your room.

You girls ok? I am mom, today is Thursday I want to come and see you both I see you are doing ok, has your mom and dad been to see you Cindy no nor yet, they will bring them later, has the doctor been here yet? Not yet it will be this afternoon, when they will make there rounds, the nurse has been here many times, giving us medicine checking our bed and other things one washed my back mom, that is nice, yes it feds better now, I am sure it does, Cindy did Sue tell you she has a birthday next Wednesday? No but remember we had her a party when she was ten years old, I gave her some socks and candy the socks came from where my dad used to work, years ago where you dad works at now Sue, I did not know your dad worked there, yes he did for five years, now he works at a gas station, he has sick pay and it has kick in now he still gets paid while he is in the hospital, that is good said Sue mom.

Sue your dad and me are going home, it is getting close to your lunch time, when your doctor comes find out how long you will be here? Ok mom, I will call later to check on you you both have a good day, take it easy so you can come home soon, we will be ok mom, I miss you so much you guess who else missing you? Bingo yes he look so sad when I feed him this morning, mom put him in my room tonight, ok I will dear, I do not want him to run away, he may go back over to Cindy, yes he might said Cindy, she was laughing, you were the reason he did that Cindy, I know I can not keep my hands of of dogs, that power man thought it was your dog, he has been there many times I guess that is why.

Ok dear we will leave, your dad has got to work tomorrow, I will see you in the morning, ok mom her mom kiss her on the face bye Cindy bye Mrs Odell you both have a good day, thank you we will you both do the same, yes mom I like it here we can talk, on the way home I thank they are doing ok, me to said her husband, she does look like she is doing good said her mom, yes she does said her husband Bob, we are here I will go see how Bingo is and make us a sandwich Bingo come here, the dog began to wig his tail ok Bingo you will be in Sue room tonight, I know you will like that, Bob here is your ham sandwich ok dear thank you so much, I will make me one, it seems so lonely with out Sue, yes it does said her husband. She has never been away from home she stay with Cindy you are right.

Sue are you asleep? Not yet why? I was thinking about what we did when we were about eight years old when we were playing one day down by the old mill we had some things we want to put them in a jar and we cover it up with some dirt, remember we said when we got older we wood come back to that place and dig it up?, it was some of our toys, yes I do remember I had a little doll and we had some things that mom gave you and me we need to go there after we get out and go get it, yes you are right Cindy, there were some of different colors, and you remember we name it colors in a web, because there was a web in a tree over the place where we put the jar, yes I do remember said Cindy, I think mom knows to, I will asked her, we did lots of things like another time we put our gum in a bottle and through it into the river next to the mill, wow you have.

Let's go to sleep, I am ready, are you? Yes I am little tired mom will be here early, dad has got to work, I know mom will come to see us, she wants to know when I will be coming home, good night Sue goodnight Cindy, the next morning Mrs Odell got up to get her husband off to work, Bob are you up? Yes I am will while you get ready I will make breakfast, ok dear, are you going to see Sue today? Yes dear I thought I would leave here at ten am spend some time with the girls, see what the doctor said about them going home, I am sure Sue ask him, will are you ready for breakfast? it is done, yes I will be there soon, ok dear I will feed Bingo come on boy he is in Sue room laying on her clothes.

Mom did dad go to work? Yes dear he did. that has be the first time he has been off work in a while, I know he must have a good time, not having to worry about going to work for two days, yes dear Sue what is the answer? When will you both get to go home, the doctor said it would depend on us, it could be a week or less we do not know, Mrs Odell I was thinking about Sue birthday Tuesday, I would loved to give her a party, yes dear, we have talk on that, her dad and me, we will do something, it is a few days we plain on going to church Sunday, your dad and me, ok mom we will cross that bridge when to get there, have you both been eating good? Yes mom we have said Sue.

Cindy has your mom and dad been to see you? Yes Mrs Odell I pray for your family, thank you Mrs Odell, will I guess I will go back home your dad will be in early, this is the day they close early, in the department he works in, ok mom you will probably get out soon, said her mom, yes I sure I will,. How is Bingo mom? He is ok he sleep in your room last night, I told you to make sure he did,. I gave him water and food this morning, thanks mom. I thank he is missing you, I know he is he does not want me to leave him every, Sue I am leaving see you tomorrow, wait mom the doctor, ok I will will girls I guess you both are ready to go home? Yes I am said Sue, ok Mrs Odell do you think you could take care of your daughter at home? Yes doctor I can. Ok she can go home, tomorrow, good said Sue thank you doctor.

She is doing good, I know doctor I left her in God. hands, good hands said doctor stone, God is the path we should travel, he will take us places we have never been before, you are right doctor, he has been good to my family, me to I never do operation until I pray, that is good said Sue mom, I will go I feel like you willl be ok, yes mom, so Sue mom left, you have a good mom Sue yes doctor I think so she has been with me through it all, she supports me doing this for Cindy, will I have made it home she hears the phone hello Mrs Odell yes this is Tom may I have a word with Sue, Tom Sue is in the hospital, what is wrong? Oh nothing she gave her friend Cindy a kidney, she did? yes Tom, you think I could go *see* her today? *Yes* you can she well be home tomorrow, I can. t wait I am going to · fort Benning Georgia tomorrow, to start my training, ok Tom she is at the hospital on the third floor room 326.

Ok Mrs. Odell, I will go *see* her today how is she and the baby? Ok I have got to make he another appointment for her to see her doctor, in a few days, I have got to see Sue I will hung up now good to talk to you again, you to Tom, you take care I wish you the best in the army, thank you *so* much bye now, will I see it is Time for Bob, I will start my beans, first I will see if Bingo is in Sue room, Bingo come here there you are, good news Sue is coming home tomorrow, you can sleep in her room again tonight, in comes her husband hi honey how was your day back at work? Ok I did get tired real easy, yes you go set down and I well get supper done, you went to see Sue today? Yes I did how is she? She is coming home tomorrow, that is good I know you will like that, yes I will, guess who called here I do not know Tom he did how is he? he is ok he ask to speak to Sue i told him what happen, he is going to see her today, because tomorrow he is going for his training that man I told you has a good head on him.

You rest Bob I will finished supper, and go clean Sue room. I will need to take care of her until she can recover, I know you will not mind taken care of her, just to have her home, you are right Bob, she was ok today, you would think she was ready to go home, you know how Sue is she has been a sport in everything she does, she has the sprite of God in her I feel, me to Bob we did carried her to church, and teach her about Jesus, I am so glad,. I know you love our little girl, she is all we have we spoiled her when she was little, what are you talking about? We still do, you are right dear said *Sue* dad, I am going and read my bible before supper, you do that dear.

Sue you have A sweet mom, I know she has been so good to me, someone is at the door come on in hello Sue are you in here? Yes come on in, Tom how are you? ok how about you ok? Why are you here? I call your mom and she told me you were here. Oh will I am glad to see you, do you remember Cindy? Yes how are you, ok Sue gave me a kidney, my was gone, she was an angel sent from heaven, I would say so said Tom, I want to see you because I will be leaving, tomorrow going to fort Benning Georgia, really Tom yes I joined the army well I wish you the best, you to Sue, let me know when you have the baby;? I will, you write me and I will write you back, Tom hug Sue God be with you Tom I will pray for you, me to said Cindy, will it is getting late I have a few places I have got to go so both of you take care he left.

Well that was a surprise, yes it was, I have not seen him in weeks, he wanted me to know he was leaving, he well be in my heart forever he was such a good person, are you sorry it did not work out for you Sue? In a way I am, I do miss him, I think of him lots, he was almost my husband, your mom and dad would not go for that, no but dad did like him and mom did to, well maybe it was not suppose to happen, you are right Cindy, he was one that made my heart skip a bet I really did care for him, Cindy you left your pie you do not wont it no I do not like apple pie to much, I do my mom will tell you that, eat it I do not wont it here take it,

Cindy remember when we asked questions about why we could not play together, now I can look back and see that did not really matter, we are still friends and that really is all that we wanted to know, why we could not play together, we know now after all these years some people still do not know, if we asked still good friend I am glad they did not know we had to work it out our self God. *s* plain not ours.

## THE END

# BOOK 2

Sue and Cindy were in the Hospital a few more days, there family came to see them and give them support. They did get out in time to give Sue her Birthday party Sue her Birthday party she turn sixteen Sue *was* a very pretty girl; Sue mom and dad asked Cindy family to move in with them, witch was ok with Cindy mom and dad, they wanted so much to go back to there on place, but they knew it was not liveable; and they were happy that Sue mom and dad offer them a nice place to live,. Sue was so happy for Cindy staying with her,. They did have a bedroom for them. And they stayed in the hospital so long they were ok to wait on there self,. Cindy and Sue they help each other, the birthday party was real nice Sue mom and Cindy mom went Shopping for the party. Sue and Cindy knew.

Everyone we are sorry but my daughter is a little tired she went to lay down. she wanted me to thank you for coming, for anyone that wants cake my friend Mrs white will help you just line up over there., the day was slow for Sue she tried to go to sleep. but could not. she had got many things from her friends. She was happy her dad got her the car. her mom went into her room to see how she was. are you ok asked her mom? Yes mom I was a little tired. but I can not go to sleep. I wanted to talk to you said her mom. Ok what is it said Sue I was thinking about you going to the doctor tomorrow, do you feel up to it? I guess, Cindy came into the room. well that was one big party. yes it was. said *Sue* mom. we did pull it off.

Cindy bought Sue some clothes. For after the Baby comes. Sue like that. All the kids came with Something for Sue. Sue mom bought the cake it was Something that Sue liked the felling was chocolate;it was a pretty pink. Sue mom made sandwich they all wish Sue happy Birthday the one thing her Daddy got her was a car he call Sue to the door he gave her the keys to a nice blue car wow said the kids. Is that yours Sue? I guess so. her dad had a big smile on his face. he told her not to drive fast. And she had to buy her on gas. that is ok dad. I do not mind. when I get out of School I well get a job. yes I wont you to go to college. I well help you until you can be on your own. thank you dad. Ok all is well said Sue mom now lets finished the party ... Mom thank you for the party. You are welcome dear. Sue was ready to lay down. mom could I see you for a minute? Sure dear. what is wrong I am not felling to good I need to lay down. Ok dear. you go and on and rest for awhile I well tell the kids you are sorry but not felling to good, ok mom.

I thank I well lay down for awhile said Cindy. yes me to mom I will try to go to sleep. ok you girls I am going to clean up the kitchen. I was wonder when mom was going to leave. I thought you were tired? No I am ok I want everyone to leave. I am not used to lots of people around. so I asked mom to say I was tired,. I knew they would leave. Cindy did you have a good time? yes I did I was asked out ... by who? you remember Billy? I told you about him wants me to go out with a few weeks ago ... what happen? I turn him Down. why Cindy? He is nice looking. yes I guess so. are you going out with him? Maybe. You should, I am thinking on it. later on Sue mom came it the room. Sue you are to see the doctor tomorrow Sue wanted to know if she could drive her new car to the doctor? Mom can I? no Sue. I well drive you in your car. ok that is ok. what time do we go I set it at ten am ok mom.

The girls went to sleep for awhile, when they got up they knew it was time to eat, they could smell the food cooking, you both sleep for a while said Cindy mom, yes we were tired. Bingo was glad to see Sue and her friend Cindy. they both played with him. Sue asked her mom to give him some food and water,. I will said her mom, Cindy mom and dad was happy to stay with the Sue family. they were talking about it while they ate there food,. Cindy mom asked about when Sue was going to the doctor she will be going tomorrow, said Sue mom, the day went by fast. rhen it was bed time, everyone it is time to go to bed, I will help you wash the dishes said Sue, no dear I will help your mom, said Cindy mom, I need to go store Friday if that is ok with you Mrs Odell. sure I need to get a few things, goodnight girls said Sue mom see you all in the morning, Sue do not forget to say goodnight to your dad, ok mom he is in the living room I will mom Sue kiss her mom goodnight.

The next day Sue mom woke her up time to go to the doctor, ok mom I well be there when I change my clothes., you hurry I do not want to be late. Cindy yes do you want to go with us? Where Sue? I have got to go to the doctor today, I have appointment at ren am oh no I have a few things to do, so if you do not mind I well stay here with mom. Ok we will be back soon, if you want to eat there is food in the kitchen. thanks Sue, see you I will take a bath first Sue left,. At the doctor office Sue sign in mom I hope the Baby is ok me to dear,. I am sure God will help you thought this, me to mom, I have faith in God, come on Sue it is time to check you, ... mom come on ok. I am coming. Sue lets get your weight first. steep up here wow you sure have not gain any weight,. how much nurse? one ten that is all? Yes now I well get your blood pressure, that is good to. your doctor well be please with you., I sure hope so,. Sue one more thing I need for you to give me a pea sample, ok nurse, when Sue finished the nurse told her to go into the room, the doctor would be with her soon ok nurse I will in a little the doctor came in how are you Sud, I see everything is ok. Lets see how your Baby is? ok doctor, will you are ok said the doctor I need to see you in two weeks, he left.

On *the* way home. Sue was talking to her mom, about *the* Baby mom its is a boy, *Sue* wanted a girl. but it did not matter because her mom and dad was the one would raise her Baby, she could put that aside. she knew one day there would be children for her. when she got married. *she* said to her self this was a mistake, but there was not anything she could do about it,. *she* wanted to make her a real good future, and put the past behind her;will Sue I am glad to get you to the doctor. and I like your car. it is better than mine, Sue was thinking you can drive it anytime you want,. I have got to get my License before I can drive, are you ok Sue? yes mom I am willl we are at home, I have got to wash some clothes before your dad gets home,. Cindy was real happy to see her best friend, she had been gone for a while..

Sue was worry about her Baby. She really want to keep it, she knew it would be better to stay with her mom and dad, she would cross that bridge when she got there, after all she had a few more months to decided on it, her and Cindy were thinking what to do with the money they found, they thought about maybe some of it could go for a store maybe a teen clothing store, that would be nice, they had talk about it many times, it was in the bank now, they had used some of it, for clothes, today is Thursday the weekend was up on them. They had to take it easy for awhile, Cindy was thinking about Billy, she really wanted to date him, he was better looking than he was when he first asked her out, it was time for bed, Sue gave Cindy a clean sheet for her bed, her mom told her to make sure she change her bed, the next day was Friday

Sue got up Cindy are you up, she did not know Cindy had made it to the kitchen.

Sue I read books and listen to folks, what I am about to tell you is your color, I am speaking of the Blacks your brothers and sisters were done wrong, by the white people, have you every notice how some of your people are dark black, and some have white in them, will when your people came from Africa to the USA, they were sold, for slavery, And many of your sisters were rape by the white man, they were real mean to them, little children were killed, your brothers were beat with anything the white man could get in his hands, it was so bad, now when the sisters were rape, the white did not want the child, they were mean to them also and if one of your brothers are sisters tried to leave they would beat them, are maybe worse kill them, the white men made them work for them, they were not to marry unless they pick there Bride, and they did not pick them from where they live, it was from someone else place, some of the white women were mean to your sisters they would live in there fancy home and the black sisters wait on them, what every they want, what they said went they did not care for you kind of people, they would burn your people out of there homes, treated them real mean, they did not want the blacks to read are write, they wont them dumb, but to me your people were more smart they there the white s, because they went to God in pray for his way, to get though every day, all they knew was work and help each other they never got to do what they want, God did not put them here to be treated wrong, he loves us all alike, they stays scared all they time, they would take a husband, from his wife and keep him for years and kids was also treated that way they did not go to School, like white., never, they would beat them to. And there mothers were treated like dogs, Cindy what are you saying, that was the way it was, I did not like what I read, are heard.

Cindy was this why they white man told me to get off the bench? I guess so I do not know, it should be over, but there is some that do not have respect, for anyone, your mother never told you anything? No why? Because she knows, so does your dad, they are old enough to remember, I guess they do not want to bring up bad memories, yes I guess *so* but I want it to come from me, not someone else, I think God took care of some of your people, they were a praying bunch of people, they had to be, to stay alive, I know they felt like no one cared, if something happen it was pined on them, weather they did it are not, they wanted to go to bed and stay, I know they were treated bad, and nothing could be done about it, you know like when you are a child and you and your brother get in a fight and your mom are dad well help you., will it was not like that, for them, why was this happened said Sue no one could put a stop to it? No Sue they lived so for in the county no one could help them the president Lincoln sign a paper to let them go, he was living for God, and I am sure he did not want that to go on, while he was president of the USA, well that was good, yes I think so I am so happy, it happened.

The next morning, Sue and Cindy got up, they were talking about going to find the things they dug a hole in the ground and buried when they were little girls, it did not take them long to find them, Sue pull the jar out of the ground, look Cindy, it has not change, you are right Sue, I put this doll in and you put its dress in, yes Sue, time sure has pass by fast, I never thought I would find this every again, me other, look Sue the web is still there, colors in a web, right over our things, yes it is, Are you ready to go? We need to get back home wow something bit me, what was it? Look Cindy it is a snake, there is a phone by the road I will call the 911 hurry Sue, you sat down, I will be right back, ok Sue, I Sue came back in a little, they are coming Cindy, thank you Sue, Cindy stay at the hospital over night, Sue call her mom and told her about what happen, she stay with Cindy, praying for her, the doctor told her mom that Cindy must have had God by her side, it was not a poison snake, she could go home the next day, thank God, said Sue.

Cindy change her mind, she told Sue she wanted to get there house in order to live in, no Cindy please don. t I want you to live with me, I can. t do that, one day I well get married and will find me a home for my family, I never thought of it like that, you to will marry one day, I want to live with my mom and dad like we were, before the storm, I miss that, I know I can get someone to work on our home and we can move back into our house, no house is big enough for to family. s, I know that is what mom and dad would wont, I am sure your mom and dad well be happy when we move., you are wrong they want you all here, yes for awhile, so I am going to get my money and get the house work on soon, ok Cindy what every you want, Sue tonight I want to tell you something ok? Sure what is it just something I know, about how the black were treated a long time ago., what are you saying?, I found out something I need to tell you, ok? we will talk tonight, ok that well be find.

Sue do you think it is time for the baby? Yes I do I well be by your side, though it all, thank you, mom are you going to call dad? Yes dear once I get you to the hospital, ok mom I am going to ask for doctor Green, well we are at the hospital, I will go get a wheel chair, come on Cindy you get the chair, I well feel out the papers, ok Mrs Odell, when Sue mom got inside, Cindy saw the chair, she went to get it, before she could get the chair, a nurse got it, Sue mom told them, Sue was in the car, need to be check, When Sue got inside, the nurse carried her to the room, where the doctor could check her, doctor green came to check her out, a little while later, Sue how are you?, well doctor green I was hurting, do you think it is time? Yes doctor green I do, well the nurse will get you ready for me, to check you, see what is going on, nurse brown get

Sue something to put on, *so* I can see how she is, in a few minutes the doctor check Sue, well little girl you will be staying here, the Baby is ready, Sue are you going to keep the Baby? Dr green my mom and dad are going to raised my Baby, well that is good, you do need to finished School, yes I do, in comes Sue mom, doctor is Sue all right? Yes she well be staying here for awhile, Sue I well call your dad, mom tell Cindy to come here, ok I well, Sue mom goes gets Cindy, is Sue staying? Yes she is, Cindy runs over to Sue, I well stay with you if you want? No that is ok, you go home, with mom after the Baby comes, ok Sue I will, Sue honey I will be back after I call your dad, ok mom I suppose he would like to be here for his first, grandchild, yes dear her mom left, Sue are you sure you want your parents to raise your Baby? Said Cindy, yes I do need to finished School, and if I did not give mom and dad permission, to raise the Baby, then, mom would take care of it for me, to finished School, she would be like mom to it, in walks Sue mom, your dad well be here soon, I thought so dad is one who makes it to me when I am in trouble, yes Sue you are his little girl, yes mom you are right said Sue, in walks nurse Brown Sue we have you a room, so lets go to 44 room you well be in bed 2 for anyone that wants to call you, I know what they well have her doing, said her mom to Cindy, she well be walking, until it is close for the Baby to be born, Cindy you go with Sue I need to call her dad again, before he leaves his work, I well be back, ok I well go to Sue room, but when Cindy got in the hall way, she saw the nurse taken Sue to the Delivery room, that is what *Sue* said, tell mom it is time, I well *Sue*.

Cindy went to look for Sue mom, she found her, Sue is having the Baby, she told me to tell you, ok I well go see what is going on, I well go with you, when Sue mom got to the Delivery room, the nurse stop her, who are you looking for? Her name is Sue Odell, she is in this room, she had a boy, are you the Grandmother? Yes is this your first grandchild? Yes it is, well you can see the Baby at that window, how is my daughter? She is fine, she came though it like a trooper, she is a sport, the Baby is fine to, can we *see* Sue now? She is asleep now, give a one hour, she well be fine, then you can see her, the Baby is in that window, if you want to see it, ok I well, come on Cindy lets go see the Baby, in walks Sue dad, where is Sue honey she is asleep said his wife Betty, has she had the Baby? Yes dear it is right here, look dear how pretty, he is, nurse could you bring the Baby to the window? So we can see him, it looks like Sue don. t it Mrs Odell? Yes it does, well dear that is our Baby, yes now we need to name it, dear why don. t we name it a Bible name? Ok we can if you want to, lets go and see if Sue is up? Ok dear, Betty did she have a hard time? No dear she came though it with flying colors, that is good, now we can go see her, she is in a different room 300 hundred, right here, there she is Betty, she looks ok, yes she does, dad mom, my best friend Cindy, how are you dear said her dad, I am ok dad, your mom call me, have you and mom saw the Baby?, yes we did said Cindy it is *so* pretty, I have not saw it yet, they well bring him to you for feeding, I am sure, mom what well you name him,? well your dad and me talk about it, I like James that is a pretty name mom, he is yours and dad. S Baby, are you sure dear, you can keep him if you like?, no mom he is yours and dad., S, honey we are going to go, it is getting late, now you rest and we all well see you tomorrow, yes Sue I well be thinking of you, I well be sleeping in that big bed, do you want Bingo to lay in your bedroom? Yes it is ok, ok dear we love you, love you mom and dad, and Cindy, see you friend they all left, the nurse came in with the Baby, here is your little man, he is going to win someone heart, when he gets older, yes I think so, Sue began to see if everything was on him, she counting his fingers and toes, and she feed him, have you come.

One the way out of the hospital, dear I have my Sue car so I well follow you, I well see you at the house, are you going to work tomorrow dear? I well call see if I can take off, so I can come with you all to see Sue and our Baby, see you at the house, when they got home Betty how is Sue she is ok, she had the Baby? great, she did that is great, so she is ok? Yes when we left she was going to rest, well I guess you both are happy it is over, yes we are, we are going tomorrow to see her, would you like to go with us?, Betty I well wait for her to come home, we saw the Baby, it sure is pretty, you know we are going to raised it, no I did not is this what Sue wants? Yes it is, it was her ideal., but she wants to go back to School, she said for us to take the Baby, and we name it James pretty name, yes we think it is. The other name, is Curtis that is his middle name, that is real pretty said Mrs White, Betty Joe and me wont to talk to you and Bob, what about? Well we have stayed with you all so long, and we thank you so much, but we want out on place, so does Cindy, that is *one* reason we want to move back in our on home, we did save a little and we are looking for, someone to work on it for us, Ruth you all can stay as long as you want to, I know that but we need our lives back again, ok if that is what you want, but if you find your self wanted to move back, come on you are welcome, I have got to call the School and let them know about the Baby, Cindy is playing with Bingo, boy you miss Sue Bingo began to bark, she had a Baby, and she well tell you all about it when she comes home.

Mom I am not to hungry, I am going to lay down for awhile, said Cindy, ok dear I want to pray for Sue, that she well come home soon, I miss her so much, I know you do dear, she well be ok said Cindy mom, Cindy went and lay down, she fell asleep and when she open her eyes the window was open, she saw the sun, I must have sleep over time, she said to her self, Cindy yes mother, Are you going with us to see Sue? Yes mother let me get dress I well be there, ok dear do you want breakfast? You did not eat your supper, I will eat later I want to see Sue, ok dear *come* out when you are ready, I'm now as Cindy went to the door, we are right behind you, said Mrs Odell, well dear I hope they don. t miss you at work,

I call they said for me not to worry, today is Tuesday, I well go to work the rest of the week, tomorrow we well get off early it is the day we clean the shop, ok dear we are at the hospital, Bob got up, this is the Baby dad he was reading the morning paper, when he lay it down, his Eyes saw the births, there in front of him was the Birth of his son born on October 20 was James Earl Odell weight five pd and 3 oz, the mother Sue Jean Odell are both doing fine, wow I am a father he was so happy, I am going to see my Baby now, he got ready, back at the hospital, Sue mother and all are going to Sue room, they knock on room 300 come on in, there Sue is with her Baby, wow I see you have the Baby said her mom, let me hold it, mom you well have to wait, until we get home its mom and dad is the only one to hold him now, ok I well wait you well be home soon, in comes the nurse, the Baby well have to go with me now, can. t be anyone in here with the Baby, ok we will see it when we leave, Sue have you heard from James dad yet? No but I feel like he well be here, why dear? Because the its Birth is in the paper, dad you read the paper, did you not see it? No your mom had me getting ready to come see you, I had the paper for one minute, dear has the Doctor been here to see you? No not yet he well make his rounds this afternoon, how do you feel ask her friend Cindy? I am ok now, Sue we well go I want to see the Baby, you call me after you see your Doctor, ok? Yes mom I well Bob is in the hospital, nurse could you point me to the where the Baby. S are? Who are you looking for, my Baby, what is its name? James Earl Odell are you the father, yes it is my Baby, come with me, at this time Mrs Odell and family come out, ok Bob, lets go see our Baby, who is that looking at our Baby? Let me see, who are you, with a big smile on his face he turn around, this is my Baby, no it is not said Sue dad, you get away, no I well not, is your name Bob yes, it is well I think you should leave, said Sue mom, why I want to see my Baby, Sue would not like it, you were only a one night stand, someone put something in my Daughter coke, that is why you are the father, Bob leaves but before he does you all have not seen the last of me.

Bob lets not tdl Sue what happen? I do not want to upset her, said his wife Batty, that is ok with me said her husband Bob, we well have to pray about this, yes dear we well said his wife well let go home, and it is getting late, we got a late start, and stay at the hospital for a long time, by the time we get home it well be supper time, I can help you with that said Cindy mom I have a few things I do need to wash, ok said Sue mom Bob I need for you to go to the flower shop get Sue some flowers, when we go to visit her tomorrow wed, I well take them to her, Cindy do not let our secret out about Bob, to Sue we do not want her to know, I well call the hospital, tell them not let Bob see Sue, ok I well not say anything said Cindy, I do not want to upset Sue, mom I am going to pray about this tell God not let Bob have the Baby, he will not tell James about Jesus, we want him to go to church, I well go now, ok dear your dad and me well go Wednesday and see if we can find someone to work on our house, Betty and Cindy mom are cooking supper, mom before I go lay down what well we have for supper? You well have to ask Sue mom this it is her house?, oh dear we well have we well have chicken and rice, green beans, and mash potatoes, and pie with ice cream sound good said Cindy, call me when it is ready mom ok I well, you go and get rest now, I thank I well call Sue first, remember do not say anything about Bob? Said Sue mom, I remember, Cindy is on the phone hello could I have room 300 bed 2 yes the phone is ringing, Sue yes how are you doing, I amok they brought me my supper and it was beans rice potatoes mash, I did not like it, why Sue? Well I did not gain any weight, they feed me like I am over three hundred pounds, no pie are ice cream, or anything that is weight gain, I want something good, well wait till you come home, we well have good food, Cindy did mom say if she saw Bob the Baby father, today, why Sue because he was here today, how do you know that?

Nurse Brown was in my room, she brought James my Baby to me and she ran, into him, he told her he was James father, hold on I well be back on Mrs Odell I am on with Sue she said nurse Brown told her that Bob James dad was at the hospital today, ok Cindy since the cat is out of the bag, you can tell her ok I well, I am back yes your mom told me he was at tbe hospital today, I though.

I call to see when you are coming home? The Doctor told me today I could leave tomorrow, if all is well. Ok I I well tell your mom and dad, call us in the morning let us know, I well we miss you so much, well the Baby get to come home? I guess so I well ask the nurse, she well know, are you going to let Bob see the Baby? That well be left up to my mom and dad, I would not let him if it was left up to me, I do not think they want him to come around, at all, they may change there minds, well I need to hung up, you get some rest, love you girl said Sue back at you, said Cindy see you tomorrow, Mrs Odell I thank Sue well be coming, home tomorrow, good she said tbe Doctor said so, what about the Baby? She is going to ask the nurse, ok Bob you well need to get the Baby bed down from, from the Attic it well go in our room, if they are coming home tomorrow he well need his bed, it was Sue at one time, now our grandBaby well have it, yes dear, I well get the cover for the bed, said his wife, what if Sue wants her Baby after she comes home said Cindy mom? Then what, well you do, I do not know said Sue mom, I guess I well give him to her, everyone is setting down to eat, when the phone rings Bob will you get the phone? Yes dear, hello dad this is Sue, hi little Girl who is that said his wife? Its is Sue let me talk to her, your mom wants to talk to you. Dad I call because James and me are coming home tomorrow, I know you work so let me talk to mom, she wants to talk to you Betty, ha how are you, Betty tell her I said I love her, your dad forget to tell you he loves you, tell him I love him mom, ok dear Bob Sue said she loves you, mom yes dear Bob was here today, I know dear, I did not want to worry you, mom I am not your little

Girl I just had a Baby, so stop putting limits on what I should know, i can handle anything, I do not need to ware children clothes I am grown, you need to cut the apron strings from, me, that *is* enough, you *well* be my little Girl forever, now when do I pick you and James up, mom you can come at twelve that well be fine, I well hung up now love you you to mom see you tomorrow.

    I have miss Sue so much since she has been in the hospital, well I guess we can finished our supper, then go to bed, if it is ok I would like to read from the bible, my wife and friends, yes sure Dear what do you want to ready,? When you all get though, I would like to read from the bible, ok dear looks like we are though, I well stack the dishes, I well help said Cindy mom, ok you all get your Bible, and I well read from Revelation chapter 7, have you all there,? Yes we are said his wife after she look around, you can go ahead dear I am reading about the mark of beast, And after these things, this is John talking, I saw four Angels standing on the four corners of the earth, holding the four winds of the earth, That the wind should not, blow on the earth, nor on the sea, nor on any trees, you family the love of God has keep some from taken the mark, our lord Jesus Christ, came to save the world, from sin, we do have a promised if we except Christ to go to Heaven, he is our way with out him we would not make it, we must let him be control of our lives, if we want to go in the rapture, and it is soon, we all know that, yes dear Joe could we get you to say a pray, before we close, yes Bob dear heavenly father we want to thank you for your word, the blood you shed for us all, thank you for the time you were well Sue when she had her Baby, and I do not want to forget our friends that let us have a place to live we love you lord in Jesus name Amen, well I guess we will all go to bed, we have a big day for Tomorrow, good night every body said Sue dad, the next day Sue is ready to go home, she is ready when her mom pick her and little James up, Cindy will you help me get my things? Sure I well, we are ready in comes the nurse, I guess you are ready, yes I am, when they got to the car bye nurse, bye Sue, hope it works out for you and your Baby, Sue has been home for awhile, when she gets a letter from Bob Lawyer about the Baby, Sue thought he had, give up on it it had been a year, James was getting big, Cindy and her family had move into there house, it was time for James Birthday party, the family of Sue had taken care of him for one year, now Bob was trying to get him since it was not a Baby any more.

Mom what are you going to do? I do not know, mom I am going over to Cindy, maybe she well know what to do, ok dear you hurry back, I want to call us our lawyer, see what he says, today is Monday I well call see if we can go to his office tomorrow, I well need to see if your Dad can go with me, when he gets home, I well call the lawyer now, give me the phone, hello Terry is my lawyer in yes Mrs Odell he is? May I speak to him? Hold on, this is Billy Brown your lawyer Mrs Odell, how can I help you I need to talk to you about Sue Baby, she has a Baby? Yes it was born a year ago, wow it has been awhile since I saw you, how is you husband? He is ok he is working all the time, well it does keep him busy I yes it does, The reason I call you it is about Sue Baby, does it have anything to do with the father? Yes it does, he has come forward since James is one year old, the lase I every saw him was, when James was born, we thought he was going to try to take him then, but he waited until James got older, now his lawyer sent Sue a letter to go to court, I see I thought it had something to do with the Baby, I well see you here tomorrow at ten PM, see if your husband can come? I well, I well talk to my husband tonight, ok see you then, *Sue* I call our lawyer and we well see him tomorrow at ten, ok mom honey don. t worry, mom I am going now to see Cindy ok dear, bye mom, see you Sue, when Sue got to Cindy she knock at the door, Cindy it is me, come on in, said Mrs White, how are you and the Baby? We are ok is Cindy here? Yes Cindy Sue is here, mom tell her to come to my room, you can go into her room, ok Mrs White, how are you Sue ok? I guess? What is wrong? I got a letter from Bob lawyer he is trying to take James from mom and dad, we are going to see a lawyer tomorrow, Sue why did he wait so long? It has been one year, I guess he did not want to take care of him while he was a Baby, you have got to pray about this I know, my dad is going to be real mad when he finds out, yes I guess so.

Cindy are you going to go with that date you told me about? Who Billy yes, well if he ask me again, why he has already ask you, why do you want him to ask you again? Sue I do not want him to think I am easy, ok I get your, point he well ask me again I believe, he may not, I well cross that bridge when I get there, Cindy do you think Bob well have a change to take James,? No I do not believe he well God is on your side, Cindy I have got to go, mom wants me home before dark, wow they sure did do a good job on this place, yes they did. I like it better, see you Sue come back anytime, Sue left, when she got her dad was there, hi little Girl, ha dad, honey we have got some bad news, your mother fell she is laying down, I need to take her to the Doctor tomorrow, we well be going at one PM she has been felling bad for a while, so I am worry, me to dad, the next morning Mr Odell go to the lawyer office Brenda we are suppose to *be* here at ten am, yes I see you are, come with me come on in Mr and Mrs Odell sec down, I have read the paper and I think we can beat this, good my wife and me are raising our grandson, we have had him a year no word from his dad, that is all we need, to know I well go to court next Tuesday, with you all, this well be a peace of cake, thank you Mr Brown, we well see you Tuesday, ok have a good day he shook there hands, and they left, now to the doctors, let me open the door I call and I am suppose to bee here at twelve am to see my doctor, yes Mrs Odell we have you for twelve, *the* nurse well be out for you, Mrs Betty would you come with me, I need to get your weight, and Blood pressure ok the doctor well see you in a little what are you here for? I fell and I have not been felling to good, this is the room you wait in, can my husband come in here? I am sorry but no, it want take long, here comes your Doctor now, Mrs Odell how are you? Not to good doctor, well I see you have lost weight, I need to put you in the hospital we well run some test, doctor I can. t I have got to to court next Tuesday, ok bur *we* do need to do the test, I will call you after court, that well be fine, tell your husband I need to see him, ok doctor sbe leaves the room Bob the doctor wants to see you, ok dear, yes doctor, your wife is real sick we need to run some test on her soon, she told me she was going to court Tuesday, yes well you make sure she comes back we took some blood, we well check that is all, so her husband leaves.

After Sue folks got out side, Betty why did you not go for the test? Bob What did the doctor say to you? He said you need to go to the hospital for them to run test on you, he is worry about you, Bob little James is important to me, if we do not go they may take him away from us, is that what you want? No that is not what I want, I love that little Boy, he is my first Grandson, I would go thought anything, to keep him with us, and I know Sue needs us too, but Betty you are important to us too, we do not want anything to happen to you, with out you I would not be able to make, it we have been married the end of this month 40 years, and I would loved to keep you another 40 years, me to dear, so lets go to court and, we need to get them test done, I agree Bob, lets fight for our Baby, then we well check me out, well we are at home, we need to talk to Sue, before you go to do them test, get out and see how our little boy is doing, Sue is wonder where we are, the week went by fast it was Tuesday, the family was getting ready for court, mom do you think, Bob well show up? Yes honey he well, he thinks he can rake little James away from us, that well never happen, said her mom and dad, as they walk in there lawyer meets them, mom I do not see Bob, she is right said they lawyer, I have been here for awhile, and I have not saw him, maybe he well not show, no luck said Sue mom, he will be here, mom they are going in, lets go, what is the case said judge Black Judge the dad is not here, where is Mr Jones? He well be here said his lawyer, here he is now, ok lets start the court, Judge I am here with Mr and Mrs Odell, with the daughter and Grandson, what they told me is Sue and Bob have a Baby that the father of little James is trying to take it from the mother, and Judge he only saw the i3aby once before it was one you old, now he is wanted to take the Baby for his own, he did not know there was a Baby, until The mother of little James told him, Sue knew it was not right to not let him know, so she look him up, now she wish she had not, Judge Mr Jones just wants to see his Baby, not take it, the Baby mom told Mr Jones she was going to give it to her mom and dad, he wants to be part of the Baby life, that is all, but her mom and dad wants the Baby, and they do not want Mr Jones to come around, he said he would pay child support, too Sue if he can see his son. He wants it to carried his name that *is* all, I have heard all of your statement, now here is what I want Mr Jones does have a right to see his Baby, and take it to his house every other week end, the Baby needs a father, this is what I want, said the judge.

Bob I think it went ok,? yes me to Betty, Sue yes was that you dad,? NO dear did you hear something? Yes dad Sue, yes hold on I want to talk to you, Sue turn around, she saw Bob the Baby dad, mom you and dad go on, here take James with you, no Sue I want to see him said Bob, lets go Bob, let the child see his dad, Sue we do not mind, ok James this is your Dad, Bob pick him up, he is a big boy, yes he is, what did you want to talk about? I am sorry the way I treated you when you came to my house, to tell me about James, I should have been more understanding, lets start over, why don. t I come by and we go for lunch, next week, I though you had a girlfriend? Not any more, we broke up, she was out to get what she could from me, you are different, thank you, so it is a date, call me before you come, ok I well, I want to learn more about you, we got off on the wrong foot, ok I have got to go, maybe I can meet your mom and dad, yes it is possible, I well call you next week, ok have a good night, you to Bob, come on James lets go, yes Daddy well see you later, when Sue got to the car, what took you so long Sue, said her dad? Dad mom you are not going to believe what just happen, what Dear? Bob ask me to forgive him, And he wants to take me out to lunch next week, really, yes dad, he was real nice to me, do you think it could be because of James? I do not know, he does not talk like he did when I told him about James, dear you need to take it slow, mom I gave James to you and dad, I know now dear if things work out for you and Bob, you need to raised him your self, don. t you think so? Mom I well cross that bridge when I get to it, we need to get to know each other, first, I agree with you dear said her mom, why do you Think Bob change his mind, he told you he would fight in court, for James, mom he did have a girlfriend, but they broke up, maybe that was the reason, he told me he was welling to marry her to keep James, honey I am not trying to tell you what to do but, watch out I smell a fish, he is moving to fast, I well mom, your mother is right I well pray about this, ok Girls and my little grandson we are at the house, Sue let me carry him for you, dad put him on our bed, ok dear, mom are you ok, I need your help Sue, dad yes? come here, ok I am, help mom she is not feeling to good, ok Betty you are going to the doctor tomorrow, you hear me, yes Bob ok then it is settle, tell her dad, only you can make her go, she well not listen to me, well she is going, Sue the phone is ringing, hello Sue yes this is Tom, I am coming home, Tom I am glad, how are you, I am ok, what about you I am fine, what did you have Tom its a boy, we name him James that is a pretty name, he is over one year old now, we just came from court his daddy try to take him from me, what happen Sue, the Judge gave him time with James every other week end, when are you coming home? About one week, call me I would like to see you ok, how is your mom and dad, they are ok thank you for asking, you tell them I said hello, I well you take care of your self, talk later bye Sue bye Tom.

Mom that was Tom, really Sue said her mom? Yes how is he dear? Mom he is ok, he call to let us know he is coming home, when said her mom? He said about a week, that is good dear, you know I said he has got a good head on his shoulder, said her dad, he said to tell you and mom hello, the next time you see him, you tell him your mom and me did not know you were talking to him on the phone, I will dad, I told him we had came from court, about James the Baby, he did ask me what did I have, I told him and we did talk about some more things, I know you were happy to hear from Sam, yes mom, I was, he has been gone long time, will everyone it is bed time, the Baby is sound asleep, he is getting so big, yes dad he is, I think he looks a lot like his dad, I me to mom, goodnight every body do not forget to say your pray, Sue mom I want but mom I am a mom now, you need to stop treating like your little Girl, you listen to *me* little Girl that will never change, I know mom but try, I need to grow up, but if you don. t help me, I never well,. I well see you both in the morning, ok dear, move over little man, the next day, it was time for Bob to get his wife to the doctor, I well be ready in a little Bob, honey you need to carry you some things, to the hospital because that is where your doctor well put you, ok Bob I well, are you ready to go? Sue I am taken your mom to the doctors, do you want to go with us? No dad I am staying here, ok dear your dad well be back in a little, ok mom, dad call me if she goes to the hospital, ok dear I well, on the way to the doctor office, Mrs Odell your doctor *is* not here so, doctor Brown well be your doctor, why is he not here? Because he had surgery, it came up all of a sudden, he knows what you are suppose to do your doctor told him, now I well get you ready to be admitted to the hospital, what well they be doing? They are going to run some blood test and other test, you well be in the hospital for one day, that is it, your doctor thinks you have a virus that is incurable we hope not, that is why we are running the test, Bob did you here that? Yes I did nurse what makes the doctor thank that? It is what he thanks, Mr Odell you can follow us to the hospital, we are taken her our self, ok I well meet you there, we have a room for her, it is 137 bed 2 she well be on the second floor, thank you nurse, she well see doctor Brown first.

When her husband got out side, I well have time to go call Sue he rang the number hello Sue this is dad, how are you and little James? We are ok dad, how *is* mom? Honey she is in the hospital by now, what is wrong with her? They do not know yet, they are going to run test on her, dad she well be ok want she? I hope so, Sue I am going to her room, she should be there now, ok dad I well be home later, kiss little James for me and grandma, I well dad, bye Sue, bye dad, Sues dad is back at the hospital, Betty I call Sue, are they ok? Yes dear, she is worry about you, I wish she would not worry, I well be find, I know you well, well have some test that the Doctor order, and we well see what they find, I do not think it well be anything, I just been worry about things, has the doctor said when you well have the test, no he want be here until morning, they are getting me ready for tomorrow, ok dear the nurse has come in, I well leave and I well call you tonight, ok dear, Bob kiss his wife bye, and left when he got home, Sue was washing the Baby some clothes, dad is mom all right? I think she well be, we do not know what it is, so we need not to worry, it may not be anything, she is not worry, I think I well make me a sandwich, do you want one Sue? No dad I will fix James something later, you come here boy, he was so busy he did not see me come in dad I can make supper if you want me to, that is ok dear, I will make me something, if I get wanted something, I told you mom that I would call her tonight, so you don't forgot and remind me, ok dad I will, boy you are getting so big, what is your mom feeding you?

Sue I am going to the store, I had the last peace of bread I need to pick up some more things while I am there, ok Dad well you get me some milk while you are out? Sure I well, I well be back soon, in a little, well I see if I can make you some soup little man, now you go seat down, while mom fix it for you, dad is getting you some milk, he well be back soon, maybe by the time.

I get your soup done, I know you ate hungry, look this is good soup I want you to eat it all, I need to call Cindy, tell her about mom, you stay here while I get your chair, let me put you in it, I know you miss your grandma, I am sure she missing you too, her and grandpa love you so much, now you seat down, I am calling my friend Cindy, so Sue calls her friend, the phone rings, hello Cindy, ha Sue, what is up,? I call to let you know my mom is in the hospital, what is wrong? They are doing test on her, tomorrow, I am so sorry to hear that, give her my love when you see her, I well her dad came in, Cindy I have got to get off this phone dad came back from the score, I ask him to pick up some milk, ok I well call you later, bye Sue bye Cindy dad thanks for the milk, ok I was glad to get it, was you on the phone with Cindy? Yes dad I told her about mom, how is she doing? Good dad, dad call mom, ok I well, give her my love and Cindy too, ok well dad I have got to put some clothes in the washer, could you look out for James while you talk to mom? Ok dear, the next day Sue dad went to the hospital, his wife was not in her room, he went to the nurse station to see where she was, nurse green said they carried her to get some test done, she would be back soon she told him to wait in her room, so that is what he did, in a little they brought his wife back, are you ok dear ask her husband? Yes I am we well know soon what is wrong with me, I prayed for you last night, I am sure you well be fine, me to dear, I hate this hospital and there hog food, it is not good at all well dear you do not have to eat it, I can bring you something if you like, no that is ok, well dear I well came back lacer, and see what the doctor says, ok dear love you Bob you to Betty, and he left, when he got home, Sue was putting James down for a nap, dear your mom has done the test, we well know something tomorrow Tuesday, I have got to go pay some bills, ok dad, I hope mom well be ok Sue was still washing while James was asleep, she went to sleep while watching TV, her son pull at her, trying to weak her up, how did you get out of the bed? Then her dad came in, I let you sleep I got James out of the bed, that is ok dad, I was about to gee him up, he did not get me up the next day Sue dad got up went to the kitchen,

    Sue hard him dad you need to get to the hospital, The doctor wants to see you, it is about mom, ok dear I will go now, I well call you later, ok dad give mom my love, I well bye Sue bye dad her dad hug the Baby and left, when he got to the hospital the doctor was in his wife room, Bob the doctor wants to tell you something ok Bob you can seat down in chat chair, MR Odell your we ran lots of test on her she does not have cancer, but she does have something it has got to do with her blood we well need to keep her for a few days, today is Friday, she can go home today but I want her here Monday, morning to take treatment for her blood, it is real low I want to start her on some iron shots, that is what wrong with her thank God it well be ok after the shots see you Monday ok doctor Brown Betty you get ready we are going home so that is what they did when they got home Sue was happy mom are you ok? Yes dear, what are you doing home well dear I have got to go back Monday, my Blood is very low is that it yes everything else is ok, thank God my prays were yes dear and your dad too he pray for me,

    Mom I want you to rest, you have been though so much, now you listen to me Sue when I was in the hospital, someone told me what to do, I am home now and this is my kitchen, I well cook the meals here, not you, as long as the good lord, gives me breath I well, take care of my self, ok mom but let me help you? If I get to weak I will call on you, betty I am going to call my job, see if I have got to be back at work Monday, ok dear you can go back if you want, no Betty I well be with you at the hospital, if they well let me, Sue the phone is ringing, I well get it., since I am close to it Betty, hello who is this? Mr Odell this is Bob, could I speak to Sue?, Sue it is Bob he wants to talk to you, ok dad give me the phone, Sue yes Bob I want to see you, tonight? What time, I well pick you up around seven, is that good for you? Yes hold on dad could you watch James for a little, Bob wants to see me, Sue you can bring James along, dad he well be going with me, ok Sue, wait Dad well mom be ok/ I wont be gone long, that is ok Sue, I can take care of your mom, I well be here for awhile, I do not know what he wants, Sue are you sure it is ok, yes dad he is ok, I am going to put James down, for awhile, James we are going to see, your dad, DA DA yes daddy you know what is going on, little man, now you go to sleep, be a good boy fur me, James close his eyes.

As the day march on Sue got her self ready, for her date with Bob, she was wonder what he wanted, that he call so soon after the court date, she really did not know, did she want to trust him? He was real mean to her the day she told him about James, was she having second thought, there were *so* many out there, that you could not give a minute, they would take a mile from you., not think twice, she began to shack, what is wrong with me, it is going to be fine, she could not say anything to her dad, he would try to talk her out of going with him, I guess I well trust him, after all it is his Baby that she well have with her, he did act like he wanted to see him, maybe I am fooling my self I well go, she got her self ready I think I well put this dress on, *it* was the *blue* dress she wear, on the TV when her and Cindy got the reward for the money, they found, it was a pretty dress, she like blue, now I have got to dress my little man, she said to her self, it was time for Bob, he knock at *the* door, her dad answer, Sue Bob is here, ok dad tell him to come in I well be there, come on in Bob she well be here I one minute, how are you Bob I am fine, I wanted to take Sue and little James out to eat I think she well like that Bob, here we are, dad I well be back real soon ok dear bye mom bye Sue, when they got out side Bob put little James in a car seat he had bought, that is nice said Sue he likes it he just had a nape, so he well be ok until we get back home.

Oh its is ok we can get a hamburger are something of what you want, I want you to give me a few minutes, ok Bob what do you want Sue we have a fine Boy that one day well be important, I believe he will be something, like a Doctor are something special, I want to be part of his life, him growing up into a fine man, he is so smart, what I am doing is, he gets down on his knees, Sue I know we have not know, each other to long but when you came to my, Apartment telling me about, lit James I just could not get you out of my mind, the fire that you have in you, when you want Something, like I tried to change your mind, about lit James saying I wanted him, But Girl you stand your ground, you told me off I like that, what are you saying I well tell you I love you and I well, do anything to make you happy, I well do what I can to be a good Daddy for our son, I know you call it a mistake when Lit James was born, but I thank God for him, I know it was not in his plain, the way it happen, but we can change things, make a good thing out of a bad, what do you say, it sounds good I well have to pray about it, I let God do my thinking for me, me to Sue, you see Sue that is another thing thar happen to me I was watching the pastor on TV when, he got to me I need something in my heart, to control what I do, chat is when I asked Jesus into my heart, that is great Bob, you see I could not marry you if you were, a sinner, I know but we can be, serving God with his help, I *love* him, and so do my mom and dad, we are born again in Jesus Christ, our lord, I well let you know Bob, now I need to go home, would you please take me,? Yes I well, I hope you, say yes, we could be a happy family, I know that James well be happy, I well call you give me your number, here it is, how did you ger my number? Out of the phone book, ok lets go, when they got to Sue, Bob kiss Sue on the lips, please let me know, I well Bob, Sue gets out Bob hugs his son before he leaves, Sue goes inside, her mom and dad are still up, how was your date dear said her mom? It was ok, what did you talk about? Nothing much, dad mom I have something to tell you, what is it dear? Bob asked me to marry him, what; I did not give him a answer, honey you are not suppose to marry a person that is a sinner, dad I am not, why do you have to think on it, if he does not know our lord Jesus Christ, that just it dad, he does he told me he got save, well that is different, if you want to marry Bob, its is up to you, he would be a father to James, and that is what your mother and me would want, are you sure dad? yes honey, Sue ran to hug her dad and mom, is that what you say mom? Yes dear like your father said it is left up to you, dad I well call Bob and ask him to come over, and talk to you and mom, ok dear you can do that, in a little while I call him dad, he well be here tomorrow night, ok dear, now it is time for bed, the next morning Sue got up she heard her mom in the kitchen this was Saturday, mom do you need help?

No dear I can do it ok I well make James breakfast, then I want to go see Cindy, her dad comes into the kitchen, dad could you watch out for James? I want to go tell, my friend Cindy and tell her I am getting married, yes dear, Sue yes mom do you love Bob? Yes mom I think I do honey when you are dating all is fun and games, now after you get married that stop, you have to to a wife job, I know mom ok.

Little boy you are staying with Grandma, mom went to see her friend Cindy, she well be back soon, now I am putting you on the couch, while I finish doing my cleaning, Bob you, look after lit James, Sue went to tell Cindy about her and Bob getting married ok dear come to grandpa, your mom well be back soon, when Sue got to Cindy she knock at the door, Cindy mom answer the door, ha Sue how are you? I am ok, how are you Mrs White? Fine how is your mom? Cindy said you told her she, in the hospital, yes Mrs white she had some test run on her Friday, and they said her blood is low, so they want her there Monday, to give her blood shots, I am sorry for her I well get over to your, place as soon as I can, give her my love and tell her I hope you gets better, ok Mrs white, I well ha Sue how are you said Cindy,? I am ok I need to talk to you, if you are not busy, ok come to my room, what is going on? I had a date with Bob, you are talking about James dad? Yes that is right, so you had a date, what happen? He ask me to marry him, what,. Yes Sue you can not marry him? Why not because he is a sinner, not any more he is save, that is good, yes I have not talk, to you since the court day what happen? He only wanted to be in James life, not take him, from me, so he stop me as mom dad and James and me lefr court, what happen before that, in court? The judge said he had a right to see his son every other week, but he call me and we made a date, well what is your answer Sue? What are you going to tell Bob, my dad and morn, gave me there blessing, *so* you are going to marry him? I think *so* Cindy, he gets along with James and he is the daddy, yes you are right, the one thing I came here for, I want you to help me with the wedding, ok I well, I have a date with Billy Tonight, really, that is good, how is your morn Sue? She has got to go into the hospital Monday, to take blood shots, I am sorry, I hope she gets better, me to Cindy, ha when is the wedding? I well let you know, when I talk to Bob, ok well I have got to go see you bye bye Sue.

When Sue arrived home, her mother met her at the door, what is wrong mom? Nothing I got a call from the pastor, he said he was having a special guest at the church, wants us to come to church, tomorrow, ok mom, I well call Bob see if he wants to go, this is at the church of God, on gore street, I remember morn we went, there with grandma Ode! I before she pass away, yes did that is true, *so* do you want to go, *yes* morn I like that church, ok we well go, I well call Bob see if he wants to go, yes dear, *so* Sue calls hello Bob yes ha Sue what up morn and me wanted to know if you would like to go to church, tomorrow, your church Sue? No Bob my grandma went there before she pass away, the pastor ask us to come, he has a special guest to preach, would you like to go?

Sure Sue I would like that, do you want dad to pick you up? No I well come by and get you and lit James, ok I well be ready around ten, ok I well be at your house ok Bob, see you then, love you Girl yes me to, have a good night, Bob you to Sue, mom Bob well pick James and me up, *so* he is going to Church? Yes mom he is, good dear, then after Church we well have time to talk, yes dear mom how do you feel now? I am ok, that is good I talk to Cindy about the wedding, is she happy dear? Yes mom I think so, she is helping me with everything ok dear, don. t you think you should tell Bob about your what you are going to do, yes mom I think so, I well tell him tomorrow, ok dear, well it is time for bed, James come on let mom give you a bath, and I well find you a suite to wear to church, let me find your little duck to play with, now here it is, take it, mom will be with you in one minute, to give you a bath, i have you sleeping clothes, Sue gives James his bath, he is happy to get a bath, now you go to sleep *so* I can go to sleep, night night little man.

The next morning Sue got up. she heard her mom in the kitchen, I see you are cooking mom, yes dear, are you and my lit grand son ready to eat? Mom I may have *some* eggs and coffee, what about toast?, yes mom I well take one peace, and I well give James some eggs to, here he is I well get his high chair, that you and dad bought him, well I have got to get ready for church, is dad going/ Sue knock on your dad door and tell him, breakfast is ready, ok mom, dad are you up? Mom has you breakfast ready, tell your mom I well, be there in a little, Bob are you going to church? Yes dear, let me dress I well be there soon as I get my clothes on, ok dear I well poor your coffee, ok dear mom Bob well come in when we get back from church, to talk to you and dad, that is ok Sue said her dad, well I am going to my room and get ready Bob well be here at ten, it is nine now, well you had better get ready said her mom, I well mom *so* *she* went to her room with James, I well dress you first, look at you, with your brown suite on, I bet your dad likes that, now mommy well get ready I well wear my blue dress, Bob well like it, now you set here while I get ready, never mind I well ask dad to watch you, dad well you keep an eye on James for me, to get ready, sure look at our little grandson Betty how sweet he looks, yes Bob he does, Sue you better hurry I hear someone out side, dad will you see? If it is Bob tell him I well be there in a little, come on in Bob Sue well be out in a little, Sue walks out wow you are sure are pretty, thank you Bob you look good too.

Are you ready Sue? Yes I am, you can carry James, come on boy said his dad, mommy sure did dress you good, you have got a really good mom, you all we well see you at church, ok dad lets go Bob, we do not want to be late for church, at church ha Sue, who do we have here? Pastor I would like for you to meet my boy friend Bob, and our Baby James, please to me you Bob, you are are welcome to God house, where is you parents Sue? They are coming-pastor, you know I miss you grandma, she, really love the lord, here comes mom and dad pastor1 hi Mrs Odall how are you all doing, we are ok pastor, glad to see you all in the house of the lord, thank you pastor happy to be here, I see Sue is all grown up, not a little Girl any more, yes pastor she is getting married, I see you are grandparents now? yes we are, James is really smart, he has brought so much love into our home, Bob lets go seat down, here this is ok, we well set behind Sue and Bob, the preacher began welcome everyone to Gods house, we do have some people with us, that had kin coming here but Mr Odell mom, pass away a while ago, I want your to welcome them here, you folks stand up, well we do have a guest with us happy for him to be here pastor Bill Brown, would every welcome him to our church, now we well have our singing, the singing was pretty, now every one lets welcome our guest pastor Bill Brown, I am so glad to be here with all of you, I was going to read from the Bible, but I just want to let you all know, that Jesus is coming soon, and I am so glad I am looking forward for his return, the lord has told me there is a lady here that needs healing, she went to the hospital for some test, and they want her to go to the hospital Monday. But she well not have to go, she well be heal, is this you he pointed at Mrs Odell?, come to me, did I speak the truth? Yes you did, the pastor pray for her in the name of Jesus be heal you see people God heal this lady, I need for you to go back for more test, and let us know what God has done for you.

Before church let out, well everyone shack hands with pastor Bill Brown, let him know how much we like his preaching, Bob are you ready to go? Yes Betty lets go Sue see you all at home, ok dad, when Sue got to the car, we need to talk Bob, can you want to talk about our wedding? Yes that is what I want, so you are going to marry me, so I well good I well make you a good husband, and James a good dad, ok we need to go to the house, and talk to dad and mom, lets go Bob kiss his waiting Bride, when they got to Sue house, dad I want you to welcome your new son law, ok that is good *so* you both want, the same, yes dad when well the date be Sue said her mom, I want to help you with every thing, you sure mom, yes dear I feel better, I am glad, sue lets set the date, ok Bob what about Christmas, we only got one month, tell we can get married, ok Bob you do not want to get married, on Christmas day no what the 23 of December, that is close to Christmas, ok I well help mom to make, plains, and Cindy wants to help, mom we are getting married the, 23 of .December, ok dear welcome to our family said Sue dad, thank you sir, mom I am going to tell Bob bye, I well walk him to the car, here give me James I well put him to bed, ok mom here he i.5 Bob kiss him before he left, well I guess we are getting married, yes I guess so see you tomorrow Sue, ok Bob he kiss her bye, he left.

The next day was Monday, Sue mom got up she was felling great, Sue met her in the kitchen, mom are you ok? Yes dear I feel fine, are you going to the hospital today? Yes dear my doctor believe in God, I am sure he well do the test over, do you want some Eggs? Yes mom and I well feed James some, he likes eggs, so he can eat with me, that is good dear, I have got to get your dad up, he wanted to go with me, mom he did not go to work? No dear he is going with me, I well call him Bob, yes dear, it is time to get up, I well be there as soon as I dress, ok dear I am ready to go, I have your breakfast ready, here is your coffee, Sue what well you be doing today? I thought I would go over to see Cindy, we well talk about the wedding, that is good dear, so Sue mom and dad left, after breakfast, come lets get you ready James, we are going over to see your aunt Cindy, now I well get ready, now I well drive us over, you have got your car seat, when they got to Cindy, Sue knock on the door, Cindy open the door, ha Sue come on in, boy you are getting so big, come to aunt Cindy, you are heavy too, Sue what are you feeding my big boy, he eats good, I would say, where is your mom at said Sue,? she had to pay some bills and dad is at work oh ok, I have something I want to tell you, what Cindy Billy ask me to marry him, are you? yes I think so, when are you and Billy getting married? Next month, that is when we are getting married, it is yes, Cindy why don. t we make it a double wedding, yes that would be good I would like that, when are you and Bob getting married? We pick the 23 of December, two days before Christmas, now what we well do is talk to Bob and Bill together, what about tonight? Ok I well call Bob and you call Bill, I can do that said Sue well got to go mom is at the hospital, she got heal, at the Church Sunday morning, that is good Sue, Cindy hug Sue bye, we well talk later James went to sleep bye little boy aunt Cindy loves you.

    At the hospital, Bob I well check in, Mrs Odell well you come with me, what are we going to do? I need to talk to the doctor, we have a bed for you, no I want to see my doctor, he well be with you in a little, here he is now, doctor yes I know you believe in God, yes I do, why because I went to Church Sunday morning, I was healed, you was? yes and I feel good, can you do the test over, sure you can come here tomorrow, and we well do it, ok Doctor, so he left, the nurse was still there, ok we will see you tomorrow for your test, Bob we are doing the test Tuesday, morning, ok we well see you Tuesday when they got home Sue was there, mom guess what, I do not know, you tell me, Cindy and Billy are getting married, really? Yes mom and I have another surprise, what dear? We are having a double wedding, I call Bob and Cindy is calling Billy, they are coming here tonight, ok dear we will go to our room, so you young people can talk, ok mom what did the Doctor say/ We will be going back to the hospital in the morning, what for? They are going to do the test over, I told the Doctor that I was heal, said we could do the test over, good mom I know every thing is ok, *so* you can look for good news, where is James Sue? Mom he is laying Down he will be up., when they get here, I think it is good that Sue and me, are having our wedding together, me to dear, you to have been friends for *so* long, and you to have been though so much together, mom I hear James he woke up, let me get him Sue, ok mom you can, I know dad and you miss him today, yes we did your dad lay down, he was so tired, come on little boy, turn them water works off, grandma has you, look Sue he is tired, yes mom I will get him some milk, he likes Bob so I am glad he is up.

Mom I am going to go clean my room, ok dear, I want to hold on to James, he is so good, to be a little boy, I remember my sisters kids, they were so mean, my sister Peggy could not handle them, I think I well call her one day see how she is since Roy pass away, I know she must miss him, mom I did not know I had a aunt Peggy yes dear she lives in Chicago, where it is real cold, I will call her one day, I would not want to go there, but I can call, it has been years since I saw her, I am sorry mom, that is ok dear, will it is getting late so it want be long until your company comes, yes mom I will go pick up the things in my room, that James put down on the floor while he was playing, mom let him down he needs to learn early, to pick up his things, oh honey he is to little for that, no he is not, so come on James, James runs to his room, ok pick them up, James puts them in his toy box, ok little man, you did a good job, I am proud of you, someone is at the door, mom there is a knock at the front door, I will get it, come on in Sue it is your friend Cindy, I am coming mom ha how are you all doing said Sue, you both can seat there, Sue I do not know if you met my Fiance, Billy? this is my best friend forever Sue we have been friends since we were little Girls, please to meet you Sue, I feel like I have know you before, Cindy talks of you none stop, yes I know that is how I feel about her, I think that may be my Fiance Bob I will let him in, ha sweet heart, sorry I am late, that is ok come on in you know my friend Cindy, this is her Fiance, Billy, please to meet you Billy said, Bob, will lets talk about the wedding, I will start with Bob, how do you feel about us all getting married,? like a double wedding for us fore? That is ok with me, me to said Billy will we all agree, yes we do, said Cindy and Sue.

Since that is settle we can go home said Cindy, yes said Billy I have got to get in bed, work comes early, nice to meet all of you, you to Billy said Bob, I will call you later Sue, ok Cindy, we will get things going on our wedding, so Cindy and Billy left, I have got to go to Sue, see you tomorrow night, Sue, ok Bob, I have got to get up early myself tell my little boy I will see him soon, ok Bob kiss Sue bye, and he left, mom dad are you up? Yes dear you can come in, dad went to sleep, but I am still up, mom it is settle, we four are having a double wedding, that is good dear, are your friends gone, yes mom the guys had to go to work, and Cindy went home to, so is James asleep? Yes mom he fed asleep while we were talking, it is late mom I am going to bed, ok dear, love you mom, love you Sue, see you in the morning, so Sue went to bed after she prayed, the next day was Wednesday Sue got up, her mom was cooking breakfast, mom did you sleep ok? Yes dear I did, what about you? Yes mom I did, good I thought you would have your wedding on your mind, yes mom I did but I prayed before I went to bed and I went to sleep, I feel fresh, me to dear, Are you going for your test? Yes I am your dad went back to work, I will drive my self, mom I can go with you, I can drive you, that is ok I will be fine, you have James to take care of, ok mom I do not mind, I know you don. t, I guess I had better hurry, mom you can get ready, I will get mine and James breakfast, ok dear I will do that, in a little her mom left, so Sue got het little boy up, time to eat, she feed him, you sure was hungry, at the hospital, one of the nurse seen Mrs Odell, you can come with me we will get you ready for the test, after it was over Mrs Oddi went to the Doctor office, I well see you Friday, the test should be back, ok Doctor, she left, when she got home, Sue was so glad to see her, all she could see was her mom in the hospital, she did not have the faith het mom had, mom is every thing ok yes dear, they want me back on Friday, mom that is two days, yes you are right, nothing wrong with me, God heal me, yes mom I believe that, ha little boy come to grandma and give me a hug, so James ran to her.

Mom you are going to spoil him., he is so mean now but I love him *so* much, I know you do dear, I need to clean my room, and James you need to pick up your things, let him down mom, ok little boy, you go help your mom, pick up your toys, James ran to his bedroom, that is right, make mom proud of you, I have got work to do my self, then we will get ready for your daddy, James was happy, he knew what his mom was talking about, the day went by fast it was time for Sue dad to come home, she saw him come up in the yard, mom dad is home, James go meet your grandpa, he is come in, James ran here comes my boy, how are you Sue? I am ok dad, mom is 9in the kitchen, well I see you have my little boy Bob, yes dear he ran to me as I got out of the truck, he is such a sweet boy, yes dad you two are not the, only ones that have spoil him, when we go over to Cindy her and her mom can not keep there hands off of him, Cindy really loves him, and he does her, well cleat you and het as friends, I am sure he would like her, Betty how was your day at the hospital?, dear I could have went with you, no I was ok I have got to go back, Friday to see how the test turn out, I already know God heal me, yes dear I think so, he knew to much of what was going on not for it to be the truth, well tomorrow is Thursday I think I have some washing to do, before I go back Friday, mom I did have a date with Bob, I am calling him and see if we can make it Friday, I well need him then, honey everything is going to be ok, you do not worry, ok mom, the night was over fast it was morning Sue could hear her mom in the kitchen, mom today is Thursday, I can wash for you I well call Cindy later.

Mom I well be back in a little, said Sue I need to call Cindy, ok dear, Sue pick up the phone she calls Cindy hello who is this? Cindy it is Sue, Sue what is up?, are you going out tonight, no why? Because I wanted you to come over and lets go over our wedding, what are we going to do we need to call the preacher, set a time when it will be good for us to have our wedding, yes well I well call the church tomorrow, there is one pretty Church that set by the lake, we could get married by the lake, I am sure the preacher well married us you know where this Church is it is on gore street, on the corner of 435 and Luke street, it is blue and white rims in the Church, very pretty I like that so I well call Friday, see who I need to talk to and we well get ready, for our wedding, ok Sue, how is your mom? She is ok she has got to go back Friday, see what the test says, that is good, that God heal her, yes Cindy I think so, Sue why don. t you come over to my house? Then we can go over what we need to do, *yes* are we having a big wedding we well talk about tonight, I well see you tonight, and bring James, are you sure Cindy? Yes I am I want to see him, we was talking about that early today, how James gets along with you, and how much you love him., yes I do, he is my little man, one day I want you to let me care for him a little, I think he would like that, I am sure he would, you spoil him to much, he likes you every Time we go to your house, he does not want to leave, I know it is like Bingo he likes coming to my house, will I have got to get off this phone, before mom notice how long I have been on here, bye Sue, bye Cindy, see you tonight ok I well drive my car there.

Sue got of the phone mom I am going over to Cindy tonight, ok dear do you want me to keep James? I would mom but Cindy ask me to bring him with me, are you sure dear, yes mom I need to take him with *me,* I promised Cindy I would, ok dear he would not be any trouble, I know mom, I well get ready, I am driving my car, dad drove it last and he put gas in it, thanks dad, you are welcome Sue, it was on empty Sue you better watch your gas, gage, I well dad, come on James lets go see your Aunt Cindy, see mom he is ready to go, Sue do you have your key?, I am locking the door yes mom I do have it, I want be out to long, I do not like leaving James in cold weather, it is a little cold, I well get his coat, see you little man, mom we well be back around eight, but do not wait up for me, when Sue got to Cindy, she knock on the door, Cindy open the door, you come in out of that cold, ha my little man, you did come to see aunt Cindy, let me hold you, mom sure dress you worm, yes I almost forgot, it was so worm at the house I change my mind when I open the door, that wind was blowing right on us, I see it is worm here, like it is at the house, mom and dad keep it worm, they do not want us to get colds, Sue give me your coat and you can seat in dad chair, they have gone to bed, I thought you had a date with Bob? I did but I broke it, it was ok, he did not mind, I told him we were having a Girls night out, what did he say about that? Nothing I think he was tired, what about you and Billy no I told him we were working on our wedding, so we can go see that church Saturday, if you want to mom is going to see about her test tomorrow Friday, at the hospital and I want to be home, when mom fines out, don. t you believe her that God heal her yes,? But I still want to be there, dad works, he wants to be there, but mom said dad work, so I will be there, ok it is settle we will, go see the Church Saturday? That is ok with me, I told mom I would hurry back, so I have got to go, don't you want anything to drink? No thank you see you Saturday, let me get James he went to sleep, I well get him, ok love you little boy your mom well have to bring you back soon, lets go boy.

    Sue got up that morning, she did not want for her mom to feel that she was along, she would stand by her, she did have faith in God that her mom was heal maybe not as much as her mom, she knew her dad wanted to be there with her mom, what every the news was, how can someone like that preacher know so much about her mom, when he had never seen her before, it had to be coming from God, I heard what he told my mom and it was true, it gave her mom faith, well I know without a thinking it is going to be fine she said to her self, I will stand on Gods promised by his strips mom is heal, I will close that subject, I have got to talk to mom, she is in the kitchen, good morning mom, good morning Sue mom how do you feel,? Ok dear will today is Friday your big day, I think everything will be ok, mom, I do to dear, has Dad left? Yes dear, he wanted to go with me but I told him to go on to work, I would be fine, mom do you want me to go with you? No dear it is nothing the Doctor, will tell me what is going on and that is all that will be said, you need to keep your mind on your wedding, call Cindy, she will help you now I am leaving, I will be back soon, ok mom God be with you thank you dear, I am not worry, her mom left, when she got to the hospital, nurse Green lead her to the doctor office, the Doctor will be here soon, she seat down, in a the doctor walk in, Mrs Odea! how are you, fine doctor, will we did the test over checking your blood and other test, I will tell you you are just fine God heal you no more test you can go home, and tell the good news to your family, so you have a nice day see you when ever, thank you doctor with a smile and tears running down her face she was happy thanking God, she went home to tell the family good news.

When she got home Sue had clean the house, mom is everything ok? yes Sue the Doctor said the test all Com back good, the Doctor was real happy for me, he said God heal me, I told you and your Dad, I was ok God heal me I felt it, I know mom, honey you did not have to clean the house, *it* is ok mom, I did not mind, well thank you, mom I see dad he drove into the yard, he must have got off early, it is not Time for him to get off,? yes mom *he* was worry about you, ha dad why are you home early? I wanted to see what the doctor said about your mom, dad let her tell you, mom tell dad, Bob the doctor said I was ok God heal me, he believe that, yes me to Betty, thank God, he did it again, where is Grandpa little man? Dad he is playing in the bedroom, James *yes* mom, Grandpa is home, you come here boy, give me a hug, what was you doing? Playing with my truck, will you seat here on my leg, I miss you today, miss you to grandpa, will I am going to read my bible Betty, I will close my bedroom door, ok dear I will have supper done in a few minutes, yes I will give some time to read your bible, the phone rings, hello Sue yes Bob I call to see if we were still on for our date? Yes you can pick me up at seven if you like, ok I will where do you want to eat? Well you remember that place on gore street, it is new, I would like to go there, yes mom and me went there one time, after they just open it up, we like it I do not remember the name, it must be good, because lots of cars were their, then we have a date,? Yes Bob see you then, love you Sue, me to, Bob hung up, mom that was Bob, we have a date tonight, yes dear, he will pick me up at seven, can you watch James? I do not want to take him, I can watch him, ok thanks mom, we wont be gone long, ok dear you all have a good time, yes mom we will, I have got to get ready, he will be here soon, I have got to call Cindy, tomorrow is Saturday we are going to check out that little Church, that is by the water, so pretty, yes dear I remember going by there one day, it is pretty, is that the place you both choose to have the wedding? Yes mom it is, the next day was Saturday, Sue was slow getting up, she went into the kitchen where her mom was making breakfast, good morning dear, did you And Bob have a good time last night,? Yes mom we did how was James? Was he good, yes dear he went to asleep, early, he was still asleep when I got home,

Mom I am getting ready to go see the church, and talk to the pastor, about performing the wedding, mom can you watch James? Yes dear, you stay with grandma, ok mom I will play with my car, let me clean your face, before I go, mom I am leaving, ok dear, when Sue got to Cindy, she notice Cindy setting on the porch, Are you ready? To go Cindy, yes I am, I am coming, Cindy the church I am talking about, is just a skip and hop from here, I can park here by the water, The lake is so pretty, I see the pastor, can I help you all? A big man was walking toward them, he had gray hair, yes sir, my friend and me want to get married, we are looking for a preacher to performer a double wedding, can you do it? I am pastor Green, when do you all want to have the wedding? We pick December the twenty third, sorry my name is Cindy, and this my friend Sue, we live a little ways from here, ok I will put your names down, thank nice to meet you have a good day, they left, I will take you home, I need to get back home to see about James, he stayed with mom, The days are passing by it is a pretty day for there wedding, mom can you do my hair? Sure I will Cindy are you ready said Sue mom? Yes I am that dress is so pretty, you are such a pretty girl, said Sue mom, thank you, mom Cindy looks pretty to don't she mom. Yes Sue she is, you both are pretty, you both go claim, your husbands lets go Cindy, ok I am ready, The wedding was so pretty, Sue and Cindy dads lead them to their waiting husbands, The pastor began to speak, we are here to joined these couples in holy matrimony, Bob do you take Sue to be your wife in sickness And till death do you part, I do, ok Sue repeat after me I Sue take Bob for my wedding husband, I promised to love him for the rest of my life till death we do part I do ok Billy and Cindy do you both promised to love each till death do you part we do, I now in Gods name pronounce that you all are husbands and wives, five years later, Sue had two children, The girl name is Sandy and the boys name is James Ray Cindy had two children Alice boy name is James Earl, Cindy and Sue took the children to the park, They wanted to talk to the Girls, you boys do your thing, us girls have got to talk, you girls seat down, while we tell you our pass, What your aunt Cindy and me went though, growing up, first of all we were playing ball, when I miss the ball, it went into the street, I went to get it got hit by a car, mom did it hurt you bad,? Not to bad they Russ me to the hospital, I was in there for a while, Aunt Cindy bought me a doll,! named after her.

Yes he did, it has been spent now, that has been awhile, then we had a bad storms that hit our county, it did not do to much to my home, but it did to your aunt Cindy, her and her family lost all they had and were in the hospital, yes Sandy I prayed for them to be ok, and finally I found them at the hospital, your aunt Cindy was real sick she need a kidney, so your mom gave her one of her kidney, you did mom? Yes she did honey, your mom saved my life, mom that is so sad, I know honey said Sue but we are real good friends, mom, yes Sandy, that means you could be sisters, yes dear, Cindy grab her and hug her yes little one we are family, now we did go though a lots your mom and me said Cindy., and you both have fore grandma and grandpa we do yes now I want you both to know, no matter what color you are, we are all Gods people, and God loves us all the same, so when you are together you and Sandy.

ARE FAMILY SISTERS LIKE YOUR MOM AND ME, WE WILL BE FAMILY TILL THE END, THIS IS MY STORY SAD NOT TRUE BUT IT SHOULD BE, EVERY ONE SHOULD LET GOD LEAD THEM NOT MAN

## THE END

www.ingramcontent.com/pod-product-compliance
Lightning Source LLC
Chambersburg PA
CBHW021427070526
44577CB00001B/89